Extraterrestrials

Extraterrestrials

What On Earth Is Going On?

**MARK HITCHCOCK
& SCOT OVERBEY**

Hearthstone Publishing, Ltd.
Oklahoma City, Oklahoma

Table of Contents

Chapter One

1996: A Space Odyssey

As we reach the millennium, the belief in the imminent arrival of extra-terrestrials in our midst is a fantasy that is as powerful as any drug, as revolutionary as any delusion that marked the last millennium, as poisonous as any great irrational upheavals of history.

The only thing needed now to make the UFO myth a new religion of remarkable scope and force is a single undeniable sighting. Such a sighting need last only a few minutes—just long enough to be thoroughly docu-mented. It will at once invest the extra-terrestrial channels, the space brother believers, and the UFO cultists with the appearance of revealed truth.

—Whitley Streiber

People in America today have an insatiable appetite for the paranormal, and the most prominent paranormal obsessions are aliens and UFOs. Consider these statistics: forty-eight percent of Americans believe UFOs are real; twenty-nine percent think we have made contact with aliens; and forty-eight percent believe there's a government plot to cover up the whole thing. According to experts, we are in a major alien moment even more intense than the *Chariots of the Gods* mania of the 1970s. It has gotten so bizarre that in one alien report recently, stargazers claimed to have seen Elvis eating fried chicken on Uranus.

The London insurance brokerage of Goodfellow-Rebecca-Ingrams-Pearson now offers coverage for that most embarrassing of risks: impregnation by an alien. Just prove that your kid's other parent came from the planet Thorg, or sprang from a chunk of Martian algae, and you can receive $156,000. The policy will pay $468,000 if you've been partly eaten by aliens, or $312,000 if you've been briefly abducted. The annual premium is a steal at $156. As one excited claims manager said: "I am looking forward to receiving details of the first claim."

We are certainly living in a "major alien moment."

Alien Invasion

Just think about all the past blockbusters featuring aliens and UFOs: *Invasion of the Body Snatchers*, *The Day the Earth Stood Still*, *2001: A Space Odyssey*, *Close Encounters of the Third Kind* and *ET: The Extraterrestrial*. Recently, there has been an unparalleled spate of movies dealing with the paranormal in general, and aliens and UFOs specifically: *Independence Day* (which was the top grossing movie of all time in the first week), *Phenomenon*, *Contact*, *Mars Attack*, *Starship Troopers*, *The Arrival*, *Sphere*, *Men in Black*, *Star Trek—The Next Genera-*

tion: First Contact, not to mention remakes of, or sequels to, *Alien, Star Wars,* and *Lost in Space.*

Even the kids have an "alien" movie to get them in on the craze. *Space Jam* features the entire Looney Tunes cast and basketball mega-star Michael Jordan. In this Disney extravaganza, Michael Jordan is transported to another realm where a group of aliens (the mean team) take on a group of NBA stars and Looney Tune characters (the toon squad). The aliens absorb the skills and abilities of the stars in an ill-fated attempt to win the game. Of course, it all turns out well and the good guys prevail, but the focus on aliens even in a kid's movie reveals how transgenerational the alien addiction has become. The idea of aliens coming to Earth in material, visible form, and drawing power out of humans is no longer "daffy" or "goofy," even for kids.

There are also at least a dozen series concerning the otherwordly on television and cable: "Sightings," "The X-Files," "The Outer Limits," "3rd Rock from the Sun," "Strange Universe," and "Dark Skies."

Cable channels offer a steady diet of documentaries, investigations, docudramas, and tabloid television dealing with every conceivable aspect of this vast topic.

In addition to all the movie and television exposure, approximately two thousand science fiction books are published each year, many of which deal with aliens, UFOs, and other strange phenomena. Disneyworld has even gotten into the fray with its new ride in the Tomorrowland area called "ExtraTERRORestrial Encounter."

The UFO mania is being further fueled by the recently alleged discovery of life on Mars. This discovery is being hailed as one of the greatest breakthroughs in modern science. Scientists maintain that if the results are verified, this will be a turning point in human history.

The so-called "Mars face" is also back in the headlines. A Viking spacecraft first photographed the face in 1976, a mile in length, staring blankly into the heavens. In the same region as the Mars face, observers have spotted other objects that appear to have smooth, angular sides like a pyramid, and what might be the ruins of walls. The recently launched *Mars Global Surveyor* is expected to send back pictures from a high resolution camera that will answer the questions as to the face's origin.

Add to all of this the hundreds of grainy photographs of flying saucers, pilot's stories of strange sightings, the rash of recent accounts of people who claim to have been abducted and subjected to bizarre physical experiments aboard "alien" craft, crop circles, cattle mutilations, and unexplainable burn marks on the ground.

All of these events and alleged discoveries seem to be coming together in some kind of paranormal convergence to focus the popular psyche of our culture on the otherwordly— UFOs and aliens.

Born on the Fourth of July

The same week that the movie *Independence Day* hit the big screen, *Newsweek* magazine (July 8, 1996) ran a cover article focusing on the explosion of the paranormal in America.

> Like more conventional religions, paranormalism has a strong millennial component. "There's going to be a boom economy in this [subject] at least until the year 2000," predicts Dennis Stacy, editor of the *UFO Journal*. Every thousand years, people expect the heavens to open up and reveal either God or little green men. *Independence Day* plays shamelessly to Judgment Day eschatology, with its fiery scenes of mass destruction, heaving dark firmament, and plague of locustlike aliens. As one of the teenagers the movie was clearly aimed at might say, "It's, like, biblical, dude." Totally. Dean Devlin, who co-wrote and produced *Independence Day,* wanted his movie to be about "how will we react at the end of the world?"

There is no doubt that we are living in the UFO generation. What was once considered wacky, hokey, and even delusional, is now accepted by half of all Americans as real. Most Americans would agree with Shakespeare's words in the tragedy *Hamlet*: "There are more things in Heaven and Earth, Horatio, than are ever dreamt of in your Philosophy."

As one writer notes,

> To most Americans unidentified flying objects are a "pop icon." The ingredients sifted, measured, and stirred into one's opinion on the subject are gathered from "pop" sources: from surface skimming programs like "Unsolved Mysteries" or made-for-TV docudramas that confess "some parts of this program are fictional" without telling us which parts. Almost without exception, these programs superimpose an extraterrestrial framework over the UFO mystery. They begin, like Arthur C. Clarke's "Mysterious World," by showing us a photo of an unidentified object in the sky. And then they ask, "Are we being watched by aliens from outer space?"
>
> The question is a "leading" one—and it's virtually the only question we've ever heard regarding UFOs.
>
> —Lint Hatcher, *Rutherford*, October 1996,p. 10

What On Earth Is Going On?

Everytime I (Mark) come or go from my house, I go through Stonehenge. You see, I live on Malvern Court in Edmond, Oklahoma, the first left off of Stonehenge Drive in the Chimney Hill addition. In spite of my close proximity to "Stonehenge," I must admit that until the summer of 1996 I was a confirmed, avowed UFO skeptic, a doubter, an unbeliever. But with all the paranormal, UFO, and alien furor, I decided that I should at least look into the subject a little just to satisfy my own questions on the subject, and the questions that others asked. However, I did not want to gather my information solely from the "pop sources." So I decided to consider the "pop sources," but also to consider other reliable writings including the most reliable of all, the Holy Bible. I ventured out on my own personal space odyssey—to boldly go where no man has gone before. I set out to discover for myself if there was really anything to all of this UFO furor and hoopla. This book is the record, or fruit, of that search that began in the summer of 1996. Let me share a few details with you about how this odyssey began and where it has taken me thus far.

Roswell

When the movie *Independence Day* hit the big screen in July 1996, I decided to go see what all the noise was about. About the same time that I saw the movie, I read several passages in the Bible that piqued my interest in this topic and for the first time led me to believe that some people may indeed be seeing something, but that they are not seeing what they think.

In August 1996, while this subject was still fresh in my mind, I had the opportunity to further investigate my germinating ideas concerning UFOs and aliens and their possible identity.

My in-laws own a vacation home in Alto, New Mexico (near Ruidoso), where my family retreats once or twice a year. When we drive there from Oklahoma, the last town we pass

The UFO Enigma Museum in Roswell, New Mexico

through is Roswell, New Mexico—the UFO capital of the world, the Lourdes of sci-fi, the epicenter of ET, the Mecca of the UFO faithful. On our trip in August 1996 I decided to take one day to investigate the UFO related sites in and around the Roswell area.

The first place I visited was the UFO Enigma Museum, which is south of Roswell on the main highway. It contains several rooms full of pictures, data, letters, official reports, and one room with a life-size re-creation of an alien ship and its inhabitants. A UFO documentary is shown in this room every hour. I was there on a Monday morning at 10:00 a.m. and every seat in the room was taken.

Next, I visited the International UFO Museum and Research Center in downtown Roswell, just across the street from the courthouse. This museum was also packed with observers. Both movie rooms were filled to capacity. The main entry room was dotted with intricate displays. The walls were papered with articles, testimonials, pictures, and data concerning UFO sightings, contact, and alleged alien abductions. The most interesting display in the museum is a very life-like rep-

International UFO Museum and Research Center in Roswell, New Mexico

lica of an alien being on a surgery table being attended by doctors and nurses. Kids were lined up at the door of this room to have their picture taken with the alien.

The museum has an extensive library and study area open to the public for further investigation and research. There is also a twenty-four–hour hotline, and counselors are available to talk with anyone who believes they have seen a UFO. While we were there, I accidentally wandered down a hallway that is off limits to the public and overheard a woman being interviewed who claimed she had seen an alien craft a few days earlier.

As fascinating as these museums were, there was one more place near Roswell that I was most excited to visit—the alleged crash site of an alien vessel in July 1947. The "crash site" near Roswell is the most celebrated shrine of modern ufology. This singular event marks the genesis of the modern UFO movement in America. It has been the subject of numerous books, documentaries, tabloid tales, an appearance on "Unsolved Mysteries," a recent TNT special movie, etc. Thousands of the "faithful" flock there every year in July to attend the annual "Roswell UFO Encounter" to mark the anniversary of the Roswell crash.

According to extensive eyewitness testimony, on July 1, 1947, radar in the Roswell, Alamogordo, and White Sands area began tracking an object that defied convention. Its speeds and maneuvers suggested that it was not a craft manufactured on Earth. On July 2, Mr. and Mrs. Dan Wilmot saw an oval object "like two inverted saucers faced mouth to mouth" passing over their house in Roswell.

An object was seen flashing through the New Mexican skies at White Sands on July 3. About 11:30 p.m. on July 4, a half dozen people living around Roswell saw an object flash through the night sky. It was bright white with a glow that looked like that from a welder's torch. In sight for only a few seconds, it fell toward the ground leaving a white trail streaked with red. During the next few days the story of an alien space-ship crash hit the press. It was the story of the century. However, the story of the century lasted only until July 9. In spite of extensive testimony to the contrary, the military quickly suppressed the hysteria by officially attributing the extensive debris field (three-quarters of a mile long and a few hundred feet wide) to the wreckage of a weather balloon and radar reflector.

While at the UFO Enigma Museum, I asked the attendant how I could visit the crash site. He gave me the card of Hub Corn, a local rancher who owns the land where the 1947 crash allegedly occurred. After talking with the attendant about the crash site and what he knew about it, I contacted Hub Corn to arrange a visit to the site. He told me to meet him at 2:00 p.m. at an arranged rendezvous point. I drove the twenty miles north of Roswell to a hot, deserted area where Hub met me in his blue Ford pick-up. Another couple was already there waiting for the tour. We waited there for a few minutes for the rest of the tour group to meet us. When the other group arrived, I discovered that it was a filming crew from Los Angeles for the syndicated show "Strange Universe." They were there to film one complete episode on the alleged events of July 1947. They had a man with them named Frank Kaufmann who was one of the original nine men from the local military base who were the first military personnel to arrive at the crash site. Mr. Kaufmann is one of only two survivors of the original nine.

We drove about eight miles from the highway on a dirt road to the impact site in a deserted arroyo. I rode with Hub Corn in his pick-up. As I walked from the pick-up toward the impact site, I took several pictures and observed the film crew making their preparations.

Upon arriving at the site, Hub told us what he knew about the UFO crash. I asked him about the visitors to the site, and he told me that he gets all kinds. He said that many people come to the site to bring flowers in honor of the aliens, that others come and fall down at the site weeping, that many psychics come there as a point of contact to communicate with alien beings, and that many come there for some kind of spiritual experience.

After Hub finished his discussion, Mr. Kaufmann shared his eyewitness account of the crash site as he saw it in July 1947. He pointed out where he saw the vessel resting and described it. It was unlike anything he had ever seen before. I listened intently as he said that it contained no fuel, but had pods underneath which experts believe somehow extracted power from the atmosphere. However, the most interesting information he shared concerned the "aliens" he observed. He told me that one humanoid-looking being about four feet tall was lying on the ground not far from the ship. He pointed out the place where he saw the being. Another being was half-

Roswell crash site

Roswell crash site debris field

Frank Kaufman (highlighted)—one of the original nine men from the local military base who were the first to arrive at the crash site in 1947. Only two of the men are still alive.

Entrance to Roswell crash site on the ranch of Hub Corn

way out of a hole in the side of the vessel, and three other beings were inside the "spacecraft." All of the beings were still and lifeless. He talked further about the disposal of the bodies and the clean-up of the debris field. He spoke matter-of-factly about the entire incident.

As I stood there on that hot August afternoon at *the* Mecca of modern ufology talking to Hub Corn, the televison producers, the other couple, and Mr. Kaufmann, I couldn't help but think about the possibility that some "alien" beings actually crashed at this place on July 4, 1947. Of course, I don't know exactly what happened near Roswell some fifty years ago, but something certainly crashed there and the military tried to cover it up. Even the Government Accounting Office admitted that in a recent report.

After reading the book *The Truth About the UFO Crash at Roswell* by Kevin D. Randle and Donald R. Schmitt I was convinced that something very unusual did happen there that stormy night in July 1947.

Incredible Journey

As a result of the current UFO explosion, my own research, and my visit to the UFO capital of the world, I was forced to ask some very difficult and perplexing questions. Could some of these alien sightings be real? If some alien sightings are real, who are these beings? Where do they come from?

These questions led me and Scot to begin our own study of this fascinating yet mysterious subject—our own personal space odyssey. Our study led us to secular experts on this subject, records of alleged sightings and abductions, ancient documents that recorded visits of alien beings to Earth, and most importantly, the Bible.

While we still maintain that most alleged UFO abductions and sightings are probably natural phenomena (bright planets or weather balloons), hallucinations, or outright hoaxes, we do believe that some people are indeed seeing something that cannot be explained. According to most experts, seventy-five to ninety-five percent of reported UFOs can be attributed to misidentified natural and man-made phenomena. However, the remaining five to twenty-five percent includes thousands of strange sightings, encounters, and abductions which simply have not been explained. UFOs have appeared in every country. There are hundreds of millions of people around the world who believe they are real. Most sightings are by "normal" people with nothing to gain as a result of their account. Even Jimmy Carter, when he was governor of Georgia, filed an official report of a UFO sighting.

As John Weldon says:

> But as far as the overall argument that there are too many physical things happening for the phenomenon to be supernatural, I'd just say the opposite: There are far too many supernatural things happening for it to be anything solely physical.

This book is a record of our own personal space odyssey where no one has gone before—our own journey to discover what these unexplained aliens and UFOs could be. Whether there are things in the Bible that could refer to UFOs or aliens. Might this be the beginning of the fulfillment of the end times? We invite you to join us on this incredible journey. It will take us to alleged sightings of UFOs, insight from the world's leading UFO experts, ancient writings such as the Dead Sea Scrolls and, most importantly, the Bible, where our odyssey will take us from cover to cover—from Genesis to Revelation. I think you will be amazed at what we discover together.

Chapter Two

Evidence That Demands a Verdict

UFOs have brought about a unique situation: hundreds of thousands of people claim to have seen something which hundreds of thousands of other people insist do not exist.

—John Godwin, *This Baffling World*

Ancient Astronauts

For thousands of years man has been fascinated with the phenomenon of unidentified flying objects streaking across the night sky. It seems that man has been experiencing close encounters ever since the dawn of time. UFO sightings have been reported in various forms since the earliest civilizations, and details of these encounters have been preserved in ancient manuscripts. From crudely painted Stone Age murals to finely detailed Egyptian hieroglyphics—from ancient papyrus scrolls to medieval paintings—it seems UFOs have been recorded in every age. For example, in the annals of Thutmose III of Egypt, who reigned between 1480–1450 B.C., it is recorded that

> a circle of fire appeared in the sky. . . . It had no head, the breath of its mouth had a foul odor. Its body was one rod long and one rod wide. It had no voice. . . . Now after some time these things became more numerous in the sky than ever before. They shone more in the sky than the brightness of the sun. Powerful was the position of the fire circles. . . . The army of Pharaoh looked on with him in their midst when the circles rose higher in the sky . . . and what happened was ordered to be written in the annals of the House of Life . . . so that it would be remembered forever.

In 218 B.C. there was a UFO wave of sorts in the Roman Empire. Strange men in white suits appeared in various places, something like a shield flew through the sky, two moons appeared at night, and mysterious luminous ships appeared in the heavens. The Roman historian Titus Livius (Livy) wrote of an unidentified object that looked like a flying altar in the sky. According to Livy this strange object flew over the city of

Hadria, Italy, in the year 214 B.C. Other Roman writers such
as Seneca, Julius Obsequens, and Joannes Lydus chronicled
the appearance of unidentified flying objects throughout the
empire.

In 329 B.C. Alexander the Great recorded in his personal
journal that he and his army were repeatedly attacked from
the sky by two objects resembling flying "silver shields." Roman author and scholar Pliny the Elder described "gleaming
beams in the sky" and how one "spark" the size of the moon
fell to Earth before rising back into the heavens again. Fiery
aerial phenomenon bearing the distinct shapes of military
shields also appeared during a battle between the Saxons and
the Franks at Sigisburg in the year A.D. 776. In A.D. 1118 it is
reported that the emperor Constantine witnessed a "fiery
cross" suspended in the sky accompanying the message, "In
this sign you shall conquer."

Chariots of THE GOD

The Hebrew Old Testament contains several accounts that
have tantalized UFO enthusiasts over the years. One of the
more interesting passages involving unidentified flying objects
reads as follows:

> And I looked, and, behold, a whirlwind came out of the
> north, a great cloud, and a fire infolding itself, and a bright-
> ness was about it, and out of the midst thereof as the colour
> of amber, out of the midst of the fire. Also out of the midst
> thereof came the likeness of four living creatures. . . . And
> they went every one straight forward: whither the spirit
> was to go, they went; and they turned not when they went.
> . . . Now as I beheld the living creatures, behold one wheel
> upon the earth by the living creatures, with his four faces.
> The appearance of the wheels and their work was like unto
> the colour of a beryl: and they four had one likeness: and
> their appearance and their work was as it were a wheel in
> the middle of a wheel. When they went, they went upon

their four sides: and they turned not when they went. As for their rings, they were so high that they were dreadful; and their rings were full of eyes round about them four. And when the living creatures went, the wheels went by them: and when the living creatures were lifted up from the earth, the wheels were lifted up. . . . And the likeness of the firmament upon the heads of the living creature was as the colour of the terrible crystal, stretched forth over their heads above. . . . And when they went, I heard the noise of their wings, like the noise of great waters, as the voice of the Almighty, the voice of speech, as the noise of an host: when they stood, they let down their wings. And there was a voice from the firmament that was over their heads. . . . And above the firmament that was over their heads was the likeness of a throne, as the appearance of a sapphire stone: and upon the likeness of the throne was the likeness as the appearance of a man above upon it. And I saw as the colour of amber, as the appearance of fire round about within it, from the appearance of his loins even upward, and from the appearance of his loins even downward, I saw as it were the appearance of fire, and it had brightness round about. As the appearance of the bow that is in the cloud in the day of rain, so was the appearance of the brightness round about. This was the appearance of the likeness of the glory of the LORD. And when I saw it, I fell upon my face, and I heard a voice of one that spake.

—Ezekiel 1:4–28

This Old Testament "close encounter of the third kind" was witnessed by the prophet Ezekiel in the year 592 B.C. Believe it or not, the Old Testament prophets were familiar with this type of unidentified flying object. In fact, several years before Ezekiel's amazing sighting the prophet Elijah was beamed aboard a similar vehicle. Listen to this incredible account found in 2 Kings chapter two:

And it came to pass, as they [Elijah and Elisha] still went on, and talked, that, behold, there appeared a chariot of fire, and horses of fire, and parted them both asunder; and Elijah went up by a whirlwind into heaven. And Elisha saw it, and he cried, My father, my father, the chariot of Israel, and the horsemen thereof. And he saw him no more: and he took hold of his own clothes, and rent them in two pieces.

—2 Kings 2:11–12

It's obvious from these accounts that at least three prominent Hebrew prophets of the Old Testament (Ezekiel along with Elijah and Elisha) witnessed unidentified flying objects. These are just two of the many biblical accounts describing extraterrestrial close encounters. We will look at these and other accounts more closely in a later chapter, but suffice it to say the Bible has much to add to our search for the truth about UFOs.

Ancient Astronauts II
One author has stated that every generation in history, except one, has recorded some reference to an unidentified object, the one exception being the generation when Jesus Christ walked the Earth, A.D. 1-30.

In his best-selling book *Anatomy*, French ufologist Dr. Jacques Vallee makes mention of several other ancient sightings:

In Hungary, spherical objects shining like stars, bright and polished, were reported going to and fro in the sky. Somewhere at sea, on July 29 or 30 in the year 966, a luminous vertical cylinder was seen. . . . In Japan, on August 23, 1015, two objects were seen giving birth to smaller luminous spheres. In August of the year 1027 at Cairo, Egypt, numerous noisy objects were reported. A large silvery disk is said to have come close to the ground in Japan on August 12, 1133.

During the period of the Middle Ages, unidentified "flying dragons" were the scourge of Europe. In the year 1492, just hours before he landed in the new world, Christopher Columbus, standing on the deck of his ship, made note of a bright object flying from the sky into the water and then exiting to return to the skies. Other strange lights were observed to be moving up and down in the distant sky.

There is the much published *Nuremberg Broadsheet,* dated April 4, 1561, which shows strange objects hurtling through the air. The sky was literally filled with cylindrical-shaped vehicles from which emerged black, red, orange, and blue-white spheres that "darted about." Historians tell us that it was "a very frightful spectacle" which was observed by "numerous men and women," in which the spheres, crosses, and tubes fought with each other for an hour until they fell to the Earth in a cloud of steam before lifting off and fading away.

In 1869 a French coin was minted depicting a flying disk-shaped object commemorating a famous UFO sighting. British astronomer, mathematician, and inventor Sir Edmund Halley (of Halley's Comet fame) witnessed a group of four UFOs in 1760, and one of them was so brilliant that Halley was able to read a printed text by its light.

Modern Ufology

The subject of unidentified flying objects (UFOs) is more popular today than it has ever been; its mounting interest to the general public has paralleled its increasing maturity and complexity. Skeptics of the UFO phenomenon were predicting in the 1950s that "flying saucers" were just another quickly passing fad. Much to their chagrin, that "fad" has become a major theme of our culture, entertainment, and social consciousness. The modern UFO phenomenon is a fifty-year pattern of steady reports of as-yet-unexplained and unidentified flying objects seen all around the globe. It seems that to our generation, more than any other, the heavens have revealed this strange, frightening, and fascinating phenomenon. These sightings have certain distinct and discernible patterns that bear no resemblance whatsoever to any technology known today. Since the initial wave of flying saucer reports in the late 1940s, there have been literally millions of sightings. While there is much that is uncorroborated, unreliable, and while there is much disinformation, there is also too much to ignore that is substantiated involving multiple witnesses. These countless sightings along with the dozens of motion pictures, hundreds of books, and tens of thousands of newspaper and magazine articles, have brought UFO sightings out of society's fringe and into the mainstream. Men and women with scientific as well as military backgrounds now talk openly and positively about the subject. There was a time when talk of flying saucers and alien visitations were considered to be topics not fit for serious discussion among sane people. Today however, the literature and lore of UFOs are receiving increased attention from all sectors of society. The governments of major nations have assembled countless dossiers about the subject.

For example, the British Ministry of Defense has publicly reversed its attitude on UFOs: it now regularly passes on UFO cases to civilian organizations and is ready to assist in providing information to researchers.

France became the first world government to create a full-time, permanent team of scientific ufologists. GEPAN (Study Group Into Unidentified Aerospace Phenomena) was launched on May 1, 1977, and is still operational today. Even the prestigious Massachusetts Institute of Technology (MIT) hosted a landmark conference on the subject of UFOs in 1992.

Phenomenon

UFO researcher Stanton Friedman refers to the UFO presence as "the event of the Millennium." "Ufology," Friedman says, "is the tumbling blood-rush excitement over the phenomenal sightings experienced around the world during this century." UFO investigator J. Allen Hynek concluded something similar in his book, *The Search for Extraterrestrial Intelligence*, when he said:

> I don't talk about UFOs very much anymore. I talk about the UFO phenomenon. The phenomenon is the continual flow of reports, now from over 140 countries. UFO reports come from highly responsible people, many of whom are scientifically trained.

Despite their long history and all the excitement, UFOs continue to remain essentially a mystery. When discussing the topic of UFOs, Wernher von Braun, the father of modern rocketry, was fond of saying: "It is as impossible to confirm their existence in the present as it will be to deny their existence in the future."

Let's examine some of the reasons why people remain skeptical to the reality of UFOs.

O, Ye of Little Faith

According to John Spencer in the *UFO Encyclopedia*, the number of UFO cases eventually solved is between ninety and ninety-five percent, with the majority of natural deceptions coming from astronomical sources, such as particularly bright stars and planets, followed by aircraft lights, weather balloons, meteor showers, and satellites. One such incident of a misidentified flying object occurred during World War II when the *USS Houston* fired 250 rounds of ammunition at Venus, while the gunnery officer kept bellowing, "Lengthen your range, lengthen your range!"

Most skeptics assert that witnesses of UFOs are simply seeing natural phenomenon such as optical illusions, plasma discharges, swamp gas, or the sun reflecting through thin atmospheric ice crystals, etc. Still others say that UFOs are nothing more than secret military spacecraft designed and operated by one of the world's super powers. All suggestions and theories to the contrary, the reality of the UFO phenomenon is becoming harder and harder to explain away.

UFO researcher Allen Hendry has reported that ninety to ninety-five percent of all UFO sightings are eventually explained as misperceptions of unusual astronomical or aeronautical phenomena, and a range of other misidentified natural and/or man-made phenomena, hallucinations, or just outright hoaxes—yet the remaining five to ten percent include hundreds of thousands of strange sightings, multiplied thousands of photographs, tens of thousands of face-to-face encounters, even alleged abductions—all of which just simply cannot be adequately explained. Therefore, the sheer weight of evidence supporting the existence of UFOs is staggering. According to UFO specialist and former chairman of the astronomy department at Northwestern University, Dr. J. Allen Hynek: "The UFO phenomenon is now a matter of fact—not just merely belief."

Something most definitely is in the air. The $64 million question is: "What?" Despite various attempts by government agencies, the military, the media, and academia to convince the public otherwise, UFOs continue to be an intriguing enigma to millions of people who believe. The space vehicles simply will not go away!

Can I Get a Witness ?

What about the people who claim to have seen a UFO? Are these reliable witnesses? Can these reports really be trusted? You be the judge!

Well, first of all, no less than thirty million Americans—fifteen percent of the current adult population—claim to have seen a UFO. It is estimated that twice that number have witnessed UFOs but have elected not to report their sightings because they fear ridicule.

A 1990 Gallup poll found that forty-seven percent of

Americans believe that UFOs are real. Forty-six percent believe that intelligent life exists in outer space. Twenty-seven percent believe that UFOs have actually touched down and visited Earth. Fourteen percent have reported personally seeing a UFO. In order to get a better idea for these statistics, think about the following comparisons:

1. For every fundamentalist Christian there are five UFO believers.
2. UFO believers outnumber Roman Catholics by a ratio of better than two to one.
3. UFO believers outnumber the voters who placed Presidents Reagan, Bush, and Clinton in office.
4. There are three adult Americans who believe that UFOs are real for every two skeptics.

Among these UFO faithful are several former U.S. Presidents. In fact Jimmy Carter filed two reports of UFO sightings while he was governor of Georgia. Paul Harvey, a reliable mainline commentator who confesses to be an evangelical Christian, reported sightings of a 350-foot elliptically-shaped object that hovered five hundred feet off the ground over a military installation in Yugoslavia. According to Harvey's report, the object traveled two thousand miles to be sighted again only four minutes later at a distant location.

Popular actor and comedian Jackie Gleason named his Peakskill, New York, residence "The Mothership" and designed it to resemble a flying saucer. Beverly McKittrick, Gleason's former wife, claims the comedian visited Homestead Air Force Base in Florida in 1973 in the company of his good friend President Richard Nixon, and that—under extremely tight security—Gleason was shown the bodies of four aliens which were allegedly embalmed and displayed on operating tables. The sight of the grotesque creatures reportedly made Gleason physically ill for days.

Prince Philip of England is considered to be somewhat of a UFO fanatic. The prince is known to meticulously chart all sightings of UFOs on a giant wall map in his private study in Buckingham Palace. U.S. Senator Barry Goldwater, a brigadier general in the Air Force Reserve, wasn't shy about his belief in UFOs. Goldwater was once quoted as saying: "These flying saucers or unidentified objects or whatever you want to call them are real."

General Douglas MacArthur, the supreme commander of all Allied forces in the South Pacific during World War II, was a firm believer in UFOs. In fact, MacArthur commissioned a report on the phenomena. The final report was over twenty thousand pages long. Near the end of his life, General MacArthur delivered a speech to the cadets at West Point in which he made the following statement: "Gentlemen, the next major war will not be an international war; it will be an intergalactic war."

Other notable men who were convinced that UFOs deserved serious consideration were President Dwight D. Eisenhower, President Ronald Reagan, and Malcolm Muggeridge of England.

"Houston, We've Got a Problem !"

NASA has claimed for years that its astronauts do not see UFOs during their space missions. However, several former astronauts have broken their silence and come forward to say that they have indeed seen UFOs. For example, the hit movie *The Right Stuff* portrayed astronaut John Glenn's close encounter with unidentified flying lights outside his orbiting capsule. In 1965 Gemini astronauts Ed White and James McDivitt made visual contact with a UFO and took several minutes of actual film footage as they orbited Earth. NASA experts estimated that the unidentified vehicle was traveling at over seventeen thousand miles per hour. The UFO was disk-like in shape and circled McDivitt's orbiting capsule. NASA has never released the White/McDivitt film. Another close encounter was reported during the voyage of *Gemini 7*. The television program "In Search of Ancient Mysteries" quoted NASA's *Gemini 7* astronauts as saying, "We have a bogey at 10 o'clock high . . ." (a bogey is an unidentified space craft). Gemini flight control quickly pointed out that the object being observed was probably just the final stage of Gemini's discharged Titan rocket booster. However, astronauts James Lovell and Frank Borman responded back that they had both the discharged Titan booster and the UFO clearly in sight.

Astronaut Walter Shirra was the first to use the code name "Santa Claus" to report a UFO encounter. Shirra observed a UFO near his orbiting *Mercury 8* space capsule.

During the flight of the STS-48 space shuttle *Discovery*, on September 15 and 16, 1991, something out of this world was sighted. To be more specific, something out of this world was recorded. A videotape shows clearly that an unidentified object was traveling near *Discovery*. Without warning it suddenly changed its course and flew away. In 1991 NASA had its own cable channel, "NASA Select," which provided live broadcasts of shuttle flights. People with access to it were able to watch the entire incident as it unfolded. Donald Ratch, of Dundalk, Maryland, recorded the flight on the downlink monitored by a local college. Later, while reviewing the tapes, Ratch noticed something unusual. There was an anomalous object rising upward from below the shuttle, traveling in a straight line from left to right and then suddenly changing direction. There also appeared to be a number of smaller, dimmer objects that followed the same path. The video shows a flash, and the largest and brightest of the objects accelerates to triple its original speed. Just after that, another object shoots upward at great speed, relative to the view on the screen.

Colonel L. Gordon Cooper, one of the original *Mercury 7*

astronauts, claimed to have chased a UFO in 1951 while he was a fighter pilot in Germany. Cooper was assigned to the 525th Fighter Bomber Squadron at Neububerg Air Force Base in Munich, Germany. While flying his F-86, Cooper saw what he described as

> an armada of flying saucers. They'd come over in pretty sizable numbers in flights like we would fly in our group formation.

Cooper said that he, as well as others, chased the saucers, but were unable to catch them. In fact, they didn't get close enough to see much detail, other than that they were metallic and saucer-shaped. On May 15, 1963, Cooper spotted a green UFO paralleling his *Mercury* space flight. Radar technicians in Australia tracked the object. Over two hundred people at the tracking station watched in amazement as the object approached Cooper's module and then sped off into space. Later in a letter he sent to the United Nations, Cooper stated:

> I believe that these extraterrestrial vehicles and their crews are visiting this planet from other planets which are obviously a little more technologically advanced than we are here on Earth.

According to Cooper: "We are being visited by aliens."

On July 21, 1969, *Apollo 11* astronauts Neil Armstrong and Buzz Aldrin claimed to have seen unusual lights in a crater near their lunar landing module. According to Armstrong and Aldrin, there were other spacecraft there and two large objects were watching them.

Apollo 14 astronaut Ed Mitchell was quoted on an April 1996 edition of "Dateline NBC" as saying: "NASA is covering up what really happened at Roswell."

Mitchell was so convinced in the existence of UFOs that

he retired from the U.S. space program in order to devote his full time to the research, study, and investigation of the UFO phenomenon.

While working on the *Mir* space station, astronaut John Blaha was recorded by HAM radio operators as saying: "Houston, this is *Discovery*. We still have the alien spacecraft under observation."

Gemini 5, 7, 8, 10, 11, Apollo 11, 12, Skylab 3, Salyut 6, the space shuttle *Discovery*, etc., have all been approached by unidentified flying objects while in space. Each time it seems that the flying objects come closer, and each time it seems that they stay a little longer.

Even NASA itself seems to be loosening up on its tight lipped policy concerning the possible existence of extraterrestrial life. For example, on August 6, 1996, NASA released the bombshell announcement of the discovery of life on the planet Mars. Seven days later, on August 13, NASA announced the discovery of water on Europa. On July 4, 1997, the United States successfully bounced its unmanned *Mars Pathfinder* onto the rocky surface of the mysterious Red Planet. NASA has also unveiled plans for a half-dozen or more additional unmanned missions to Mars, following in the footsteps of the *Pathfinder* and the *Mars Observer*. What about the possibility of man walking on the surface of Mars? Scientists say it's not a question anymore of "if," but rather "when." Most scientists agree that man will land on Mars sometime around the year 2005. Why all of the fuss about possible life on Mars? Why are we spending so much money on the search for extraterrestrial life? Perhaps Orson Welles answers this question best:

The discovery of just one bacteria on Mars or any other body of the solar system would indicate that the whole chain of evolution—cosmic, chemical, and biological—is at work everywhere. In that case, the creation of life anywhere in

UFO photographed by Ella Louise Fortune, October 16, 1957, as it hovered over Holomon Test Range, New Mexico.

the universe would be more the rule and not the exception. In that case there may be other intelligent civilizations capable of communicating with us. The impact on ourselves given the advent of contact with another intelligent civilization—how it might come about and what the effects might be—is one being discussed by serious thinkers the world over. The more we study the evidence that is being assembled from all over the Earth, the more inescapable the conclusion becomes that man should prepare himself for the greatest event in human history—the realization that we are about to contact or be contacted by beings from another universe.

Believing Is Seeing

The variety of UFO witnesses is exhaustive. The list includes men and women from every possible rung of the social ladder. Not just crackpots, psychos, or lunatics, but normal family men, many of whom held responsible positions in their communities at the time of their sighting. There are the countless military witnesses from the Army, Navy, Air Force, and

Marine Corp who are radar technicians, guided missile launchers, control tower personnel, base commanders, ground troops, engineers, pilots, and weather observers. To an unprejudiced investigator it would be hard to find a better qualified, more distinguished group of witnesses to observe and report on the existence of UFOs.

The list of UFO witnesses includes astronomers, astronauts, cosmonauts, state, county, and city police officers, photographers, FBI agents, private pilots, as well as pilot crews from every major commercial airline. Poll after poll shows that about one-half of the American public believes UFOs are something real, and about twenty-five percent believe that UFOs are alien spacecraft. Millions of people in Russia, the United Kingdom, Australia, Mexico, France, South America, Canada, and other countries around the world have claimed to have witnessed UFOs.

World renowned UFO researcher Jacques Vallee claims to have in his personal files cases of "close encounters" from every country on Earth. In their book *Flying Saucers Are Hostile,* Brad Steiger and Joan Whriteow give the account of phenomenal sightings in Russia:

> In the spring of 1959, UFOs brought more panic to the Soviet radar and air force personnel by hovering and circling for more than twenty-four hours above Sverdlovak, headquarters of a tactical missile command. The Soviet fighter pilot sent aloft to chase the UFOs away reported that the alien objects easily outmaneuvered their jets and zigzagged to avoid their machine gun fire. Dozens of nervous candidates for Soviet civilian flying licenses have complained about UFOs sweeping at them and even following their planes back to airfields. Two Russian cosmonauts returned to Earth in March 1978, after ninety-six days in orbit aboard their *Salyut 6* orbiting spacecraft and reported of a formation of UFOs which trailed them closely for three complete

orbits around the globe. One of the cosmonauts filmed a twenty-minute motion picture of the encounter. A second camera took still shots, securing outstanding pictures. Unofficial statements from NASA state that it is the best footage ever filmed of UFOs.

On the July 16, 1996, edition of "ABC Nightline," the topic of discussion was a recent UFO sighting by the United States Air Force. The title of this particular program was "Are We Alone?" The program began by showing amazing footage of two streaking UFOs taken by United States Air Force cameras. The following is an excerpt from the program:

Ted Koppel: The U.S. Air Force photographed these objects, but they have no idea what they are. By definition that makes them UFOs, unidentified flying objects . . .

Michael Guillen (ABC News science correspondent): The sighting you are now watching was recorded by a powerful Air Force telescope high on the mountaintop on the island of Maui. The unmanned-robot telescope was scanning the sky, looking for orbiting space junk, when suddenly, these bright objects appeared. The Air Force declined to comment officially, but a key officer involved in the sighting says that these are probably nothing more than airplane lights.

Dr. Robert Nathan (scientist at NASA's Jet Propulsion Lab and UFO skeptic): It seems highly unlikely that these are airplane lights. If it were an airplane, I think we would see, as it moved across the screen, that the body of the airplane in front would obstruct the stars as it moved, and as we examine this thing, the image, it doesn't seem to have that effect. Therefore, I think it's a set of objects which are glowing from being burned up in the atmosphere.

Michael Guillen: Could this be a flying saucer, or several?

Dr. Robert Nathan: It is an unidentified flying object, but that doesn't mean it's an alien craft. There's just not enough information to make a pure judgment.

Dr. Bruce Macabee (Navy physicist): This thing is going much too slow to be a meteor, unless you assume that it's so high up it's beyond the atmosphere. However, if it was above the atmosphere it would not be glowing as it is—you would be unable to see it. Meteors don't glow in space. Meteors only glow when they strike the atmosphere.

Michael Guillen: So, does this sighting intrigue you?

Dr. Macabee: Oh, yes! And this would have to rank up at the top, in terms of credibility, and pretty far up there in terms of strangeness.

This Air Force sighting is just one of the latest additions to the galaxy of UFO sightings recorded over the past fifty years, all of which fuel America's skyrocketing fascination with the subject.

Born Again Believers

Over the past fifty years unidentified flying objects have been tracked on radar, plotted on multiple radar simultaneously, fired on by Air Force jets, photographed, and filmed. The mountain of evidence pointing to their existence is so massive that Marcia Seligson, writing for *New West Magazine*, has said: "There is now an accumulation of material evidence weighty enough to bury even the toughest of skeptics."

Dr. J. Allen Hynek, past chairman of the Northwestern University astronomy department agrees:

> There is now sufficient evidence to suggest that we are not alone. It is no longer possible to sweep away the whole subject of UFOs. I can establish beyond a reasonable doubt that they are not all misperceptions, hallucinations, or hoaxes.

It is interesting that Dr. Hynek was himself once an avowed UFO skeptic. According to Dr. Hynek:

Before I began my association with the Air Force and Project
Blue Book, I had joined my scientific colleagues in many a
hearty guffaw at the psychological postwar craze for flying
saucers that seemed to be sweeping the country and at the
naivete and gullibility of our fellow human beings who were
being taken in by such obvious nonsense. When I first got
involved in this field, I was particularly skeptical of people
who said they had seen UFOs on several occasions and totally incredulous about those who claimed to have been
taken aboard one. But I've had to change my mind. It is no
longer possible to sweep away the whole subject. It reminds
me of the days of Galileo when he was trying to get people
to look at the sun spots. They would say that the sun is a
symbol of God; God is perfect; therefore the sun is perfect;
therefore spots cannot exist: therefore there is no point in
looking.

Although once a staunch UFO skeptic, Dr. Hynek, after years
of intensive and exhaustive research, came to the conclusion
that most UFO reports are from "reliable, excellent witnesses."

One such reliable witness was Clyde W. Tombaugh, the
astronomer who is credited with the discovery of the planet
Pluto. One night during the summer of 1948, Tombaugh was
sitting in the backyard of his home in Los Cruces, New Mexico.
Dr. Tombaugh, along with several witnesses and members of
his family, watched in amazement as a strange glowing craft
moved overhead. All of the witnesses agreed that the object
was definitely a solid ship—some form of extraterrestrial device.

Edward J. Reppelt, one-time head of the the Air Force's
Project Blue Book had this to say about proving the existence
of UFOs:

What constitutes proof? Does a UFO have to land at the
entrance to the Pentagon, near the joint-chief-of-staff of-

fices? Or is it proof when a ground radar station detects a UFO, sends a jet to intercept it, the jet pilot sees it, and locks on with his radar? . . . Is it proof when a jet pilot fires at a UFO and sticks to his story even under the threat of court-martial?

Silent Majority

Another fact one must consider when attempting to wade through all the UFO data is that ninety percent of the people who claim to have seen a UFO never report the incident. These people make up what UFO expert Dr. Hynek calls "the Legion of the bewildered silent."

However, those who do report UFOs average some one hundred and fifty sightings every twenty-four hours.

Group Think

It should also be noted that many UFO sightings are often witnessed by dozens, hundreds, and even thousands of people at the same time. Are we to believe that these are just cases of mass hysteria? According to Dr. Stanton Friedman, nuclear physicist and UFO researcher: "It would be strange indeed if all this evidence were the result of mass hysteria." Dr. Friedman contends that:

> There is a multi-witness Close Encounter of the Third Kind occurring somewhere on this planet every day. This is in addition to the Close Encounters of the First and Second Kind.

One such multi-witness, mass sighting occurred over the skyline of Indianapolis, Indiana, on July 13, 1952. A massive oval-shaped craft was spotted moving very rapidly over the city. The speeding object was clearly visible to thousands of stunned spectators. Immediately, police switchboards, telephone operator boards, newspaper offices, and radio stations were bombarded by calls from hysterical citizens. At the exact same time, Air Force radar personnel had locked in on a high-flying craft matching the size and speed of the object seen by citizens of Indianapolis. Furthermore, pilots from Eastern Airlines, American Airlines, and the U.S. Air Force all testified that they made visual contact with the craft as it traveled over the city at a phenomenal rate of speed. Mass hysteria? Group hallucination? UFO expert Ian McLennan says:

> Hundreds of thousands of people cannot make independent observations of the same optical phenomenon over thousands of square miles under some kind of fantastic dose of mass hysteria.

Sacred Ground

Like any emerging movement, *ism* or *ology*, ufology has its own unique set of holy shrines. Examples include Kirtland Air Force Base, with its crypts of mystery; Dulce Air Force Base, New Mexico, with its great temples; Groom Lake, Arizona, with its secret hangars; and Roswell, New Mexico, with its famous debris fields.

We must remember that ufology is very much a technocratic movement, therefore its sacred shrines are not places like Jerusalem, Bethlehem, Mt. Sinai, etc. Ufologists designate their holiest of sites by the use of code names—locations like Area 51, Majestic 12, Hangar 18. It is on a pilgrimage through this sacred landscape that I now invite you. Truly something does seem to be happening out there. And it seems to be increasing in its frequency as man approaches the year A.D. 2000. Let's take a closer look now at some of the more famous unexplained UFO sightings of all time. Ufologists would tell us to remove our sandals now because we will be standing on holy ground.

Chapter Three

Sightings

The First Wave

A UFO is the reported sighting of an object or light seen in the sky or the land, whose appearance, trajectory, actions, motions, lights, and colors do not have a logical, conventional, or natural explanation, and which cannot be explained, not only by the original witness, but by scientists or technical experts who try to make a common sense identification after examining the evidence.

—Dr. J. Allen Hynek, director of the
Center for UFO Studies (*CUFOS*)

I saw a disc up in the air
   a silver disc that wasn't there.
Two more weren't there again today
   Oh I wish they'd go away.

—Words written on the bathroom wall at the
White Sands Missile Range in New Mexico

The Mother of All Sightings

The modern UFO era began in the mythical summer of 1947. This would be the sighting that started it all. Ironically, it was just one year before the death of Orville Wright, coinventor, with his brother Wilbur, of the first "flying machine."

In the early afternoon hours of June 24, 1947, Kenneth Arnold, a 32-year-old Idaho businessman and experienced pilot, was flying his single-engine *Callier* across the majestic snow-covered Cascade Mountain range in Washington State.

Kenneth Arnold

It was a crystal clear sunlit day and Arnold was heading east toward Yakima, Washington. Several days earlier, a Marine Corps C-46 transport had disappeared over Mount Rainier with thirty-two men on board. Arnold, who was a member of the Ada County (Idaho) Aerial Posse, as well as an acting deputy federal United States marshal, and a member of the Idaho Search and Rescue Mercy Flyers, was playing the part of "rescue pilot," hoping to collect a $5,000 reward for locating the missing plane and its crew. According to Arnold, June 24 started out just like any other ordinary day.

> I had just finished installing some fire fighting apparatus at Chehalis, Washington. The job finished, I began a chat with Herb Critzen, chief pilot for Central Air Service. We talked about the possible location of the lost Marine transport which had gone down in the mountains. I decided to look for it. It meant a $5,000 reward, and I hoped that via my proposed route to Yakima, Washington, I might be lucky enough to find it. I decided to spend some time in the air in the vicinity of Mount Rainier to make a good attempt at locating the wreckage.

Arnold never did find the missing Marine aircraft that day, but he found something else instead—or, maybe it found him.

As Kenneth Arnold searched the 14,400-foot-high plateau of Mount Rainier, suddenly, according to Arnold, "a tremendously bright blue-white flash lit up the surface of my aircraft." This initial flash was followed by a second and then a third. Arnold's attention was drawn by this series of flashing lights off to his left. At first Arnold thought that there had been some kind of colossal explosion. Arnold took a quick glance at his watch, which read just a few minutes before 3 p.m. As Arnold fixed his gaze in the direction of the flashes (Mount Baker) he saw an amazing sight.

> Nine very bright objects coming from the vicinity of Mount

Baker, flying very close to the mountain tops. I was fascinated by their formation. They didn't fly like any aircraft I had ever seen before. In the first place, their echelon formation was backward from that practiced by our Air Force. The elevation of the first craft was greater than that of the last. They flew in definite formation but erratically, darting in and out of the smaller peaks, periodically flipping on their sides in unison.

Arnold went on to explain that these strange looking aircraft were moving across the sky at an incredibly high rate of speed. Using some quick calculations, Arnold estimated their speed at well over seventeen hundred miles per hour—nearly three times faster than any jet currently in operation.

Another characteristic of these craft that made a tremendous impression on me was how they fluttered and sailed, tipping their wings alternatively and emitting those very bright blue-white flashes from their surfaces. At the time, I did not get the impression these flashes were emitted by them, but rather that it was the sun's reflection from the extremely polished surface of their wings.

As Arnold focused in on the streaking squadron, he couldn't help but notice their odd shape. A crescent-shaped object led the formation, while the rest of the craft were disk-shaped. Arnold, an experienced pilot with well over four thousand hours of flying experience, had never seen anything like this. Arnold realized that these craft defied any technology of which he was aware. Awe struck by the silvery disks, Arnold continued to track them for the next four minutes. Arnold was especially fascinated by the fact that he couldn't "find any tails on them."

As the nine objects flew out of sight, he unsuccessfully tried to explain them out of his mind as some sort of top-secret technological wonder belonging to the Air Force. "They made me feel eerie," Arnold explained. Somehow the $5,000 reward money didn't seem so important to him any more. According to Arnold: "I wanted to get to Yakima and tell some of the boys what I had seen."

When Arnold landed for his brief stop in Yakima at 4 p.m., he excitedly described what he'd seen to some people on the ground. The first person he confided in was good friend Al Baxter, general manager of Central Aircraft. Baxter found the report hard to believe. However, Baxter knew Ken Arnold to be an honest man. According to Baxter:

> Kenneth Arnold was neither crazy nor the type to pull a stunt—he was in fact a level-headed character and an experienced pilot. Besides, he had nothing to gain from making up such a story, and everything to lose.

Word of Arnold's encounter spread like wildfire. By the time Arnold had flown on to his final destination of Pendleton, Oregon, he was mobbed by a swarm of newspaper and radio reporters. Everybody wanted to know more about the strange machines he had sighted. Back on the ground, Arnold told reporters that the chain of nine peculiar aircraft had moved very erratically. Arnold guessed that the unidentified objects had been some twenty miles away from his airplane. If he was right, it would mean that their size would have been enormous. Experts estimated that at that distance even the largest aircraft ever built would have been impossible to see without binoculars. Arnold said that the objects had been flying diagonally in echelon formation, dipping and skimming across the contours of the mountain range. According to Arnold:

> They were approaching Mt. Rainier very rapidly, and I first assumed they were jet planes. Anyhow, I discovered that this was where the bright flashes had come from, as two or three of them every few seconds would dip or change their course slightly, just enough for the sun to strike them at an

angle that reflected brightly on my plane. As they approached Mt. Rainier I observed their outline against the snow quite plainly.

When asked to describe the movement of the strange disks, Arnold struggled for just the right words:

> They were like speed boats in rough water. . . . They were like the swooping tail of a Chinese kite. . . . They bounced through the air in a most unusual way . . . like geese in a diagonal formation . . . flat like a pie pan and so shiny that they reflected the sun like a mirror. They flew in a rather diagonal chain-like line, as if they were linked together.

Finally, Arnold said, "they flew like a saucer would if you were to skip it across the water."

Arnold's choice of words would prove fateful. Bill Bequette, an Associated Press reporter who had been scribbling down the story as fast as he heard it, latched onto the word "saucer," and so was coined a phrase known the world over: "flying saucer."

Bequette wrote his story, telling the world that aerial intruders had arrived. It was the scoop of the decade. Little did Kenneth Arnold know that the modern age of the UFO had just been born. This was the beginning of uforia. From that moment on, newspapers were filled with stories of the flying disks and flying saucers. The "flying saucer" would grip the popular imagination. The genie was now out of the bottle and the evening sky would never be quite the same again.

The bold headlines of the next day's *Seattle Post-Intelligencer* declared: "Mystery Disks Hurtling Across the Sky."

Kenneth Arnold, a rescue pilot, fire fighting equipment salesman, and trusted solid citizen, came across as a man of honesty and integrity. His story was believable. An American historian of the period wrote:

The floodgates were now open for the rush of reports that was soon to follow. But it had taken a man of Arnold's character and forthright conviction to open them.

Lint Hatcher, writing for the Rutherford Institute points out:

> Arnold's sighting was the beginning of something new, even revolutionary. There had been very little talk of visitors from outer space during earlier reported sightings. Most sightings up to this time had been described as "airships" rather than "spaceships." The Zeppelin-like airship scares of the 1800s generally were attributed to German spy machinery or to anonymous inventors straight out of a Jules Verne novel. The Arnold sighting, on the other hand, was immediately discussed in terms of extraterrestrial visitors.

Kenneth Arnold had become ufology's archetypal ancestor, its primal progenitor, its "First Man." For weeks after the sighting, the Arnold home in Boise, Idaho, was besieged by reporters seeking additional information about the nine mysterious craft.

> I can't begin to estimate the number of people, letters, telegrams, and phone calls I tried to answer. After three days of this hubbub I came to the conclusion that I was the only sane one in the bunch.

On June 27, United Press International wired this report to its affiliates about the world's most famous saucer sighter:

> PENDLETON, Ore., June 27 (UPI)—Kenneth Arnold said Friday (June 27) he would like to get on one of his 1,700 mile-an-hour "flying saucers" and escape from the furor caused by his story of mysterious aircraft flashing over southern Washington.

Each year since Kenneth Arnold's legendary sighting, UFO enthusiasts have made their pilgrimage to the foot of Mt.

Rainier. They gather there to commemorate the event that marks the birth of the age of the flying saucers, and maybe through an exhibit of sheer faith, nudge along their return.

Also, it is interesting that for twenty-five years the New Age Foundation has held their annual UFO convention near the famous Mt. Rainier site. Large groups of UFO faithful gather for several days before and after the June anniversary date of Arnold's sighting at a spot they call SPLAASH, an acronym for the Spacecraft Protective Landing Area for the Advancement of Science and Humanities. Today, many still feel that the site is a "contact point" for alien visitors.

In the beginning, the critics were slow to attack Arnold. But eventually the critics surfaced. Donald H. Menzel, a professor of astrophysics at Harvard, who was later to become a professional saucer-skeptic and debunker, said that Arnold had been fooled by tilting snow clouds or dust haze reflected by the sun. Others said that the objects Arnold sighted were due to a mirage. In 1981 Arnold told ufologist Greg Long:

> These nameless, faceless people ridiculed me. I was considered an Orson Welles, a fraud. I loved my country. I was naive about the whole thing. I was the unfortunate goat who first reported them.

Arnold, however, stuck fast to his story, and the item made the front-page of newspapers across the nation. According to Arnold:

> The story of what I observed over the Cascade Mountains, as impossible as it may seem, is positively true. I never asked nor wanted any notoriety for just accidentally being in the right spot at the right time to observe what I did. I reported something that I know any pilot would have reported. I don't think that in any way my observation was due to any sensitivity of eye sight or judgment than what is considered normal for any pilot.

Critics accused Arnold of everything from seeing clouds to seeing an optical illusion or perhaps an aerial mirage. Some critics even accused Arnold of borrowing the image from a book such as *War of the Worlds*. Arnold eventually stated that he regretted going public with his sighting, claiming: "I wouldn't report a flying ten-story building after the way I was treated by the debunking press and skeptical public."

However, the very same day Kenneth Arnold made his observations, as many as eighteen other sightings of strange flying objects were reported in the Pacific Northwest. There were 850 sightings reported during the months of June and July alone. In the six months that followed Arnold's sighting, Air Force researchers found 156 UFO reports worthy of further study. In fact, the very same morning of June 24, a prospector named Fred M. Johnson had spotted five or six "round, metallic-looking disks" about thirty feet in diameter and about one thousand feet above him. Johnson estimated that he watched the disks for over a minute through his telescope. Johnson claimed that during the sighting his compass needle spun wildly, stopping only after the disks headed off.

A Gallup poll of August 19, 1947, less than two months after Arnold's sighting, revealed that nine out of ten Americans knew about the flying saucers, whereas considerably fewer had heard of the Marshall Plan for the postwar reconstruction of Europe. The age of the saucers had arrived!

Apparently sightings of silvery disks had been going on since April of 1947, when a U.S. Weather Bureau meteorologist and his staff had tracked a large flat-bottomed ellipsoid as it streaked across the skies above Richmond, Virginia. UFO experts claim that similar sightings took place during the months of June and July in the states of Oklahoma, Colorado, Tennessee, Georgia, and New Jersey. The wide news coverage of public reports of "flying disks" or "saucers" created sufficient concern at high military echelons to authorize the Air Materiel Command to conduct a preliminary investigation into these reports. In the summer of 1947, the Air Materiel Command was asked to study the situation and make recommendations about what should be done. On September 27, 1947, Lieutenant General Nathan F. Twining, the AMC head and commanding officer at Wright Patterson Air Force Base, notified the Pentagon: "The phenomenon reported is something real and not visionary or fictitious." Three months later Washington was concerned enough to launch Project Sign, issuing orders to the Air Force to collect and evaluate "all information concerning sightings and phenomena in the atmosphere which can be construed to be of concern to national security." By the late 1940s Air Force investigators had begun to call such craft "unidentified flying objects" (UFOs).

Whatever Kenneth Arnold saw during his infamous flight over the Cascade Mountains in 1947, he retained his passion for the subject of UFOs right up until his death in 1984. This would suggest that his experience was something much more tangible than just imagination. An FBI agent who interviewed Kenneth Arnold right before his death made the following statement concerning the veracity of Arnold's claims:

> It is the personal opinion of this interviewer that Mr. Arnold actually saw what he states he saw in the attached report. It is also the opinion of the interviewer that Mr. Arnold would have much more to lose than gain and would have to be very strongly convinced that he actually saw something before he would report such an incident and open himself up for ridicule that would accompany such a report.

The swirl of interest and excitement surrounding the Kenneth Arnold sighting would scarcely have time to run its course before another major skyquake would come crashing onto the Earth's scene—this time near Roswell, New Mexico!

Above Top Secret
The Roswell Crash
This is the granddaddy of them all. It is world famous. It all

started here. A patch of desert outside of Roswell, New Mexico. This is ground zero for the modern UFO craze. The Roswell incident of July 1947 is believed to be the single most significant incident in UFO history—the one that many believe will eventually prove an alien presence on Earth. Back in 1947, witnesses say that a flying saucer crash-landed there, and to this day, fifty years later, they're still talking about it.

The Roswell crash has been written about in this country by a myriad of authors; it has been featured on more television shows than Madonna; and it was the subject of an original cable television movie. As if that were not enough, Roswell played a central part in the plot of the major blockbusting movie of the summer of 1996, *Independence Day*. Roswell has been featured on "Star Trek: Deep Space Nine"; is mentioned frequently on the mega-hit TV series "The X-Files"; and has turned up in all sorts of arenas including *Penthouse* magazine, where the first alien centerfold appeared. It is impossible to write a UFO book today without mentioning **Roswell**.

Only two weeks after Kenneth Arnold saw what the press first called "flying saucers," a startled world heard the news

Front page of the *Roswell Daily Record,* July 8, 1947

that one of the flying disks had crashed. On July 8, 1947, Lieutenant Walter Houtt issued a press release for the Air Force, announcing that it had indeed recovered a flying disk just north of Roswell, New Mexico. But the following day, after creating an international sensation, the military reversed itself, saying the debris found was merely the remains of a crashed weather balloon. To this day, Lieutenant Houtt vehemently denies the weather balloon story:

> The weather balloon story was strictly a cover-up. I really believe that it was a flying disk. Honestly, I think it was the collision of two craft.

The Roswell story begins on Friday, July 4, 1947, when James Ragsdale and his girlfriend, Trudy Truelove, started their three-day weekend by driving north out of Roswell on old Highway 48. Ragsdale and Truelove had planned a weekend of "camping." Ragsdale turned off the main highway and continued down the back roads until he and Truelove were far away from the city lights. That night turned out to be anything but quiet as a powerful thunderstorm whipped across the desert terrain. According to Ragsdale, at approximately 11:30 p.m. "brightness flashed as an object roared overhead."

Ragsdale said that the object he observed was a flaring bright light, blue-gray like that of an arc welder. At first he thought it was a lightning strike not far from him, but then he caught sight of the object itself as it blasted directly over his campsite. Seconds later Ragsdale heard the thunderous crash as the object slammed into the ground about a mile or so from his camp.

When the storm finally ended, Ragsdale convinced Truelove that they should go look for the thing that crashed. Ragsdale and Truelove drove across the rocky terrain and came to the edge of a small cliff. There they saw the remains of a strange ship stuck in the side of the cliff. With their small

Roswell crash model in UFO Enigma Musuem—Roswell, New Mexico

flashlight failing, the two decided to head back to camp and return to investigate further the next morning.

Early the next morning Ragsdale and Truelove ventured back to the crash site. In the daylight Ragsdale got his first good look at the object that had crashed into the ground. It looked like part of an aircraft with narrow wings. Part of the strange craft was buried in the side of the cliff, while the other part was angling out of the ground. Ragsdale also saw what resembled bodies. According to Ragsdale "they were not very long . . . four or five feet long at the most. They looked like midgets."

Ragsdale's survey of the crash site was cut short by the arrival of military personnel who immediately cordoned off the area. Ragsdale and Truelove hid in a nearby stand of trees and watched as the military began to clean up the debris field. According to Ragsdale: "They cleaned everything all up. I mean they cleaned it. They raked the ground and everything."

Another witness to the crash was William Woody, who lived just south of Roswell. Woody was watching the sky with his father when he spotted a fast moving white light with red streaks in it. The light glowed brilliantly and was unlike any of the meteors he had seen in the past. Woody watched the object descend and disappear just north of Roswell. The time was 11:30 p.m.

In the town of Roswell itself at Saint Mary's Hospital, Fran-ciscan Catholic nuns Mother Superior Mary Bernadette and Sister Capistrano were making routine night observations when they saw a brilliant light plunge to Earth due north of their location. They believed the object to be some kind of disabled aircraft and recorded the sighting in their logbook on the night of July 4 between 11:00 and 11:30 p.m.

At exactly the same time a group of archaeologists in the Roswell area also saw the strange blue-white object in the sky. They watched it plummet to the ground. They made plans to search for the crash site first thing the next morning.

The archaeology team led by Dr. W. Curry Holden from Texas Tech University came upon the crash site around dawn on the morning of July 5. The craft, according to one of the archaeologists, looked like a crashed airplane without wings. It had a fat fuselage. As the archaeology team approached, they also made the grisly discovery of three strange looking bodies. Two of the bodies were lying outside of the craft and one body was visible through the hole in the side. The archaeologists believed they were looking at some type of experimental aircraft. Dr. Holden directed one of the students to go back to the main highway and alert the local authorities concerning their discovery.

Another eye-witness to the Roswell crash was Corporal E. L. Pyles. On July 4 Corporal Pyles was on assignment south of Roswell. Pyles recalls looking up into the night sky and seeing what he thought at first was a shooting star, but larger. It moved across the sky and then arced downward. There was an orange glow around it, a halo near the front. According to Pyles, the object seemed to be heading for a crash landing somewhere north of town.

Military officials were also aware that something strange had happened that night outside of Roswell. Military radar technicians had been tracking an unidentified flying object over southern New Mexico since July 1. The object had first appeared over the highly restricted area near White Sands Missile Range about one hundred miles from Roswell. White Sands, of course, was the sight of the first atomic bomb detonation in 1945, and currently the home of top secret missile research.

On the night of July 4 the object as depicted on military radar began to pulsate, with the blip growing larger and brightening before shrinking to its original size and dimming. This activity kept up for a short period of time and then the object blossomed into a sunburst and disappeared from the screen at about 11:25 p.m.

Ballard's Funeral Home in Roswell plays an important part in the puzzle surrounding the alleged UFO crash. Ballard's received a call around 1:30 p.m. on July 5 from the Roswell AFB mortuary officer who began to ask a series of strange questions. According to Glenn Dennis, a mortician working

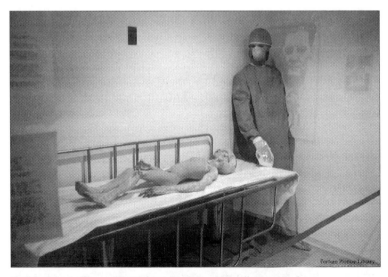

Model of dead alien at UFO Enigma Museum—Roswell, New Mexico

at Ballard's, the officer was asking about what size and what types of caskets were available and how small they were. The officer was also interested in caskets that could be hermetically sealed. Thirty or forty minutes later, Dennis received another call from the same officer asking about preparations— preparing a body that had been laying out in the elements and how would they treat burnt bodies or the very traumatic cases. Dennis walked the officer through the steps on how they treated those types of cases.

But the mortuary officer wasn't through yet. According to Dennis, the next question was: What would be done in a case where you didn't want to change any of the bodily chemical content—where you didn't want to destroy any of the blood—where you didn't want to destroy anything that might be important down the road?

Interviewed over forty years later Dennis said:

> I knew at the time that something had happened . . . something they probably weren't ready to release. . . . I told them I could come out and help them, but I was told that this was for future reference.

Scores of other witnesses, including military personnel stationed at the crash site, all tell of a top-secret operation to remove the remains of the crashed alien craft as well as the remains of the dead alien occupants. Even today, some fifty years after the fact, startling evidence continues to be uncovered. Top-secret government documents have become available, and eyewitnesses have stepped out of the shadows after years of fear-induced silence to provide further evidence that a UFO did indeed crash on July 4, 1947, outside of Roswell, New Mexico.

At the Roswell Police Department there is what is reported to be a piece of the downed spacecraft's instrument panel on display. Max Littell, curator of the International UFO Museum in Roswell, says that the piece of metal was analyzed at New Mexico Tech University, and the interesting thing about it was that they found out it was made up of copper and silver. After fifty years, the copper has not corroded and the silver has not tarnished.

As a result of all of this explosive data, tourists have been arriving in droves to experience Roswell first hand. Visitors with aliens on their minds account for one-fifth of the hotel business and pump an estimated $5 million into the economy every year, say Chamber of Commerce officials. Each year since 1993 Roswell has been host to the UFO Encounter Festival. The festival drew twelve thousand humanoids in 1996. However, July 1997 was the fifty-year anniversary of the Roswell crash and city planners put on a festival that surpassed all that had come before.

Organizers estimate that some 250,000 people beamed into Roswell between July 1 and July 6, 1997, spending money on hotels, restaurants, souvenirs, and dozens of events. By February 1997 all of Roswell's estimated one thousand hotel rooms were completely booked. The city promoted lodging within a ninety-mile radius and cleared several acres for campers and RVs. The '97 festival featured an all-night rock concert (who else but the "Foo Fighters" and the "Stone Temple Pilots"), lectures by paranormal experts, alien abductees, crash site investigators, and UFO experts of all kinds were available. Visitors who plunked down an additional $70 were allowed to attend a banquet held in an original hangar like the one in which the alien corpses were reputedly stored in 1947. Hourly bus tours took people to one of four alleged crash sites. Other events included costume contests, a Flying Saucer Pancake Eating Contest, a Flying Saucer Soap Box Derby, a Crash and Burn Extravaganza (a parade down Main Street showcasing vehicles modeled after alien spaceships), films, symposiums (speakers included Erich von Daniken, author of *Chariot of the Gods?*), and even a group of UFO belly dancers.

Chapter Four

Sightings II

The Truth Is Out There

What power urges them at such terrible speeds through the sky? Who, or what, is aboard? Where do they come from? Why are they here? What are the intentions of the beings who control them? Before these awesome questions science—and mankind—can yet only halt in wonder. Answers may come in a generation—or tomorrow. Somewhere in the dark skies there may be those who know.

— *Life Magazine,* April 7, 1952

The First UFO Martyr

At approximately 1:15 p.m. on January 7, 1948, the control tower at Godman Field Air Base in Kentucky received a telephone call from the Kentucky State Highway Patrol inquiring about an unusual aircraft that might be being tested in the area. Residents of Marysville, Kentucky, had flooded the switchboard at highway patrol headquarters with reports of a strange aircraft flying over their city. Within minutes, residents of Owensboro and Irvington, Kentucky, were reporting similar sightings. At 1:45 p.m. the control tower at Godman Field made visual contact with the bright disk-shaped object which they were unable to identify. Commanding officer Guy Hix, along with five other officers and an aide, watched the gigantic metallic object, its top glowing a crimson-yellow, hover over the airfield. Control tower personnel quickly determined that this craft was not an airplane or a weather balloon.

At 2:30 p.m. Commander Hix along with base intelligence officers and other high-ranking personnel were discussing what to do about the object when four P-51s were seen approaching the base from the south. Captain Thomas Mantell, the flight leader, peeled off in pursuit of the UFO after the tower asked him to attempt to identify the craft. Within minutes Mantell claimed that he "had the thing directly in front of him." Captain Mantell was still in a steep climb at ten thousand feet when he made his last radio contact with the tower: "It looks metallic and it's tremendous in size. It's above me and I'm gaining on it. I'm going on to twenty thousand feet."

These were Mantell's last words. His wingman saw him disappear ominously into the dark clouds. Air National Guard captain Thomas F. Mantell, Jr., died when his F-51 crashed after giving chase to what he called, in one of his last radio transmissions, "a metallic object of enormous size." The official Air Force line was that Mantell had unfortunately been killed while trying to give chase to the planet Venus.

Did a distant planet really lure this experienced pilot to his death? Had the residents of Kentucky and the experts at the Godman Field control tower been observing and tracking a planet? Any astronomer will tell you that it is next to impossible to see Venus against a clear blue sky in the middle of the day—and even if you could see the planet, it would definitely not look like a rapidly moving, metallic object of enormous size.

The events surrounding the tragic death of Captain Mantell set off a controversy that still rages today. There were reports of a closed-casket funeral because of the mysterious wounds on Captain Mantell's body; there are even reports that Mantell's body was never found. Whatever the truth, the United States Air Force had once again found itself entangled in the enigma of unidentified flying objects.

Mantell is recognized today as the first martyr in the annals of ufology. The legend of Captain Mantell is that of a brave young pilot that, while protecting his country, was shot down by a hostile UFO and the military is hiding the truth.

The Eastern Airlines Incident

At exactly 2:45 a.m. on July 24, 1948, veteran Eastern Airlines pilot Clarence S. Chiles and copilot John B. Whitted spotted an object that at first appeared to be a distant aircraft. But it was moving much too fast. Just seconds later the craft raced past them at incredible speed. As the craft passed, Whitted saw what he described as

> a huge, tube-shaped structure, its fuselage three times the circumference of a B-29 bomber, and with two rows of square windows emanating white light. The underside had a deep blue glow, and there was a fifty-foot long trail of orange-red flame which shot out the back.

Chiles and Whitted were positive that it was not the planet Venus they were seeing. Chiles was a former wartime lieutenant colonel in the Air Transport Command, with eighty-five hours of piloting to his credit. Whitted was also a military veteran and an expert in B-29s. Captain Chiles recounted how the craft shot past them quickly, rising some five hundred feet and then disappearing into the clouds at about six thousand feet. "It pulled up at a tremendous rate of speed, with a burst of flame from the rear. Its prop wash or jet wash rocked our plane."

The unidentified craft was also viewed by one of the non-sleeping passengers aboard the DC-3. The passenger was Clarence L. McKelvie, a managing editor of the American Education Press. These witnesses were highly experienced air crew who were backed up by one of their passengers. Their testimony carried considerable weight.

Unknown to Chiles and Whitted, a ground maintenance crewman at Robbins AFB, Georgia, had spotted an identical aircraft only one hour earlier. The object had a phosphorescent glow and was moving horizontally—exactly as the Eastern Airlines crew had described. The day after the sighting, FBI boss J. Edgar Hoover received the following notification from Strategic Air Command in San Antonio:

> An unidentified flying object was seen by an Eastern Airlines pilot and co-pilot and one or more passengers while flying over Montgomery, Alabama. The unidentified craft was reported to be of an unconventional type having no wings. The object resembled a rocket ship like in the comic strips. It had windows and was larger than the Eastern Airlines jet and was traveling at over twenty-seven hundred mph. The craft narrowly missed a collision with the Eastern Airlines jet.

Four days earlier stunned observers at The Hague, the Netherlands had observed a similar tube-shaped object moving rapidly across the night sky. U.S. Air Force investigators said that this case "shook them worse than the Mantell incident."

Foo Fighters

Following the "classic" sightings of Kenneth Arnold, Captain Mantell, and the Eastern Airlines pilots in 1947 and 1948, not to mention the hundreds of other similar but lesser known sightings, many Air Force pilots were reminded of the bizarre "foo fighters" which many Allied personnel had seen during World War II. During the war thousands of Allied aircraft were flying missions above Europe and the Pacific on bombing raids, reconnaissance missions, and other operations. Never before in the history of mankind had so many people been above the clouds, scanning clear skies with eagle-eyed intensity. It is hardly surprising that the UFOs, which had probably always been there, were now being spotted in abundance.

Often on bombing missions both pilot and crew would spot strange glowing lights that would shadow their bombers. They were nicknamed "foo fighters," after a nonsense phrase used by a cartoon character by the name of Smokey Stover ("Where there's foo there's fire"). "Foo" is also the French word *feu* meaning "fire." Sometimes the "foos" would flutter and dart in and around their aircraft. Other times the "foos" would be seen flying in formation. At first the lights were assumed to be St. Elmo's fire, electrical discharges appearing in the form of balls of light around pointed metal objects. St. Elmo's fire is commonly seen on the wingtips of planes or the mastheads of ships. But flight crews were insistent that they had seen St. Elmo's fire elsewhere and that this phenomena was nothing like it. But as the reports continued to pour in, so did the uneasiness that the glowing balls of light might be hostile. Air crews began to realize that something strange was going on. One Air Force major, a B-17 pilot with over fifty

missions under his belt, told journalists about his experience
with the "foos":

> Suddenly they'd be on our wing, six or eight of them, fly-
> ing in perfect formation. You turn and bank, they turn and
> bank; you climb, they climb; you dive, they dive—you just
> couldn't shake them. Little dirty gray aluminum things, ten
> or twelve feet in diameter, shaped just like saucers; no cock-
> pits, no windows, no sign of life. . . . When the things got
> tired of the game, they would just take off into space and
> disappear, flying at the most incredible speeds, five thou-
> sand miles an hour or more.

B-17 pilot Hilary Evans reported a sighting on October 14,
1943, when a bomber raid on an industrial plant at
Schweinfurt in Germany was mounted by the American
384th. On their final bombing pass many crew members observed a "cluster of disks" dead ahead. The disks were "silver
colored, about one foot thick and three feet in diameter." According to the crew, they were "gliding down slowly in a tight
group."

The most widely reported sighting occurred on November 23, 1944, and involved an American fighter unit based
out of France. Lieutenant Edward Schlueter was flying from
Dijon on an intercept mission to Strasbourg and Mannheim,
flying mostly above the Vosges Mountains. With him were
Lieutenant Don Meyers and an intelligence officer, Lieutenant Ringwald. It was Ringwald who first made visual contact
with the what he later described as "ten balls of orange-red
fire moving at great speed in formation." The sky was clear
and Ringwald was an excellent and experienced observer. The
crew debated the nature of the strange lights. Were they
misperceptions of stars? Meteors? Reflections? The crew dismissed each possibility and decided to go on the offensive. As
the American fighter closed in, the fireballs simply melted

into nothingness. Minutes later they reappeared, then vanished again. It was if they were playing tag.

Retired Air Force major Paul Deutch described a similar encounter while flying over Japan:

> The particular one that we saw was an orange-red color that trailed our aircraft for miles and miles. Our top gunner on the B-29 bomber fired a burst of machine gun fire. We saw the tracers go directly toward it—they seemed to go directly into the object, but nothing happened. At the time we thought it was a Japanese secret device probably developed by the Germans, and I might add that pilots in the European theater thought it a was a German device— the Germans thought it was an Allied secret weapon—everybody thought it was somebody else—nobody knew what it was.

Many similar sightings followed. Most military personnel classified the "foo fighters" as some type of Nazi secret surveillance device or secret weapon. However, not a single "foo" was ever shot down or captured. The "foos" were sighted in both the European and Far Eastern theaters. Radar stations and on-board radar in the aircraft showed that nothing was actually there. Yet the lights chased bombers, and proved more than a match for them with incredible displays of speed and maneuverablilty. Some of the best military pilots in the world found themselves outmaneuvered.

Official censorship kept reports of these phenomena out of the newspapers until December 1944. By the end of the war it was discovered that German and Japanese pilots had also been tailed by the strange lights. It came as a surprise to thousands of pilots when the Air Force officially decreed that the mysterious lights had "never" actually existed at all—it had been nothing but a case of mass hallucination. This report was, of course, not believed due to the fact that the reports of the "foos" existence were coming from the most reliable, eagle-eyed pilots in the world. It is also reported that the "foo" phenomenon was present later in the Korean and Vietnam wars as well.

The Lubbock Lights

During a two-week period between August and September 1951, thousands of residents of Lubbock, Texas, witnessed a spectacular light show in the west Texas sky. Four professors from Texas Technical College (now Texas Tech University) observed the glowing string of bluish beads flying in a crescent formation. The "Lubbock lights," as they came to be known, were estimated by the professors to be traveling back and forth at speeds in excess of eighteen hundred miles an hour.

A nearby Air Defense Command radar station picked up the UFOs flying at thirteen thousand feet at over nine hundred miles per hour. College student Carl Hart, Jr., observed the formation of eighteen to twenty white lights through his bedroom window. The lights flew in a perfect boomerang-shaped formation. Hart grabbed his parent's 35mm camera and raced outside, quickly snapping five pictures. A local newspaper as well as the Air Force closely scrutinized Hart's photographs of the "Lubbock lights." After intensive investigation, no evidence of a hoax ever emerged. One observer was quoted as saying: "All Lubbock ever had was Buddy Holly and the lights, and now they've only got the lights."

Disappearing Act
November 23, 1953
On the evening of November 23, Air Defense Command radar was frantically tracking an unidentified target moving at five hundred miles per hour above the waters of Lake Superior. As radar technicians tracked the object, an F-89C all-weather jet interceptor from Kinross AFB took off in hot pur-

suit. As the crew approached the UFO they reported back to ground control that they had spotted the craft, and described it as circular in shape and bright bluish-white in color. They then chased the UFO over Lake Superior at speeds in excess of five hundred miles per hour. Radar operators watched the jet close in on the UFO, and then something unbelievable happened—the two blips on the radar screen merged. The F-89 and the UFO were locked together. Moments later both vanished from the screen, and all communication between the base and the interceptor ceased.

The Air Force launched an extensive land and water search but found no trace of the jet or the two men aboard. The bodies of Lieutenant Felix Moncla, Jr., and radar observer Lieutenant R. R. Wilson have never been recovered. The Kinross incident remains a UFO encounter of the strangest kind. One radar operator was reported as saying: "It seems incredible, but the unidentified blip apparently swallowed our F-89."

Fender Benders

The first reported collision of a UFO and Earth vessel occurred on April 1, 1959, near McChord Air Force Base in Washington. In this incident, the pilot and two crew members were all killed.

Lieutenant-Colonel Robert Bowker of the U.S. Air Force had just such a near miss with alien technology in 1950 while flying from Wake Island to Honolulu. According to Colonel Bowker:

> Red lights in a pattern came up on the port side and spun the medium-frequency AADF (on-board electronic navigational equipment) so fast I thought it would be destroyed and turned it off.

Several months later Colonel Bowker recalls that he had to comfort the pilot of a C-54 inbound from Wake Island to Hickman Air Force Base on the island of Oahu. According to

Bowker: "He was shook up so bad I had to help him hold his whisky glass." The pilot reported that eight glowing red objects had shot straight at him, closing in at over one thousand miles per hour. Just before impact, four had passed above and four below his aircraft. Both the C-54 pilot and Bowker were warned by an NSA (security) officer to remain silent about this top-secret encounter. Bowker was pretty sure that he now knew what UFOs were and that those officers in the twenty-eight security levels above "top secret" were in possession of a lot more data about UFOs.

Another mid-air collision occurred in 1960 over Wisconsin. This time there were seven persons aboard the plane, but only two bodies were found. The other five had mysteriously disappeared into thin air. It is interesting that in all of these collisions there was apparently no damage to the UFOs.

A fourth and more recent collision case occurred over the Bass Strait, some 130 miles south of Melbourne, Australia. Frederick Valentich was piloting his Cessna 182 when he spotted an unusual object approaching from behind. When Valentich first made visual contact with the strange craft, he radioed the Melbourne Flight Service Control and described his pursuer as a "green light and sort of metallic on the outside." As the object closed in, Valentich radioed that he could see four bright lights. Control tower personnel recorded Valentich's last words as follows:

> It isn't an aircraft, . . . Melbourne. . . . It's approaching from due east toward me . . . flying at a speed I cannot estimate. It is a long shape. Cannot identify more than that. . . . Coming for me right now. . . . The thing is orbiting on top of me. My engine is choking.

A metallic scratching sound then replaced the pilot's voice, only to be followed by complete silence. A few seconds later Valentich and his aircraft disappeared for good.

Lost in Space

A kissin' cousin to the mid-air collision variety of UFO sightings has been the baffling cases which report the complete disappearance of Earth vessels which leave no trace. Over the years, both airplanes and ships have disappeared, never to be seen or heard from again.

The most famous of these disappearances occurred in the infamous Bermuda Triangle. On December 5, 1945, a squadron of five Avenger torpedo bombers with fourteen experienced crew members flew out of Ft. Lauderdale Naval Air Station in Florida. It was a short, routine flight. Each plane had a full load of fuel and weather conditions were excellent. All five planes were in good mechanical order, including all instrument panels, equipment, and engines. Each of the aircraft had been painstakingly preflighted, and each plane carried an extensive array of radio gear, including ten communication channels, plus homing devices. To top it all off, each aircraft was equipped with a self-inflating life raft, and each of the experienced pilots wore a Mae West life jacket. But despite all of the safety precautions, something strange happened. Things began to go wrong. The flight leader radioed in and reported not having any sense of direction. The control tower then ordered the squadron to head due west. The leader, with alarm in his voice, responded:

> We don't know which way west is. Everything is wrong. Everything is strange. We can't be sure of any direction— even the ocean doesn't look as it should.

The pilot then stated that "weird unidentified aircraft were closing in on him." The pilot's radio unexplainably went dead and all five airplanes disappeared without leaving a trace.

A giant Martin Mariner with a crew of thirteen was dispatched to search for the five missing planes. The Mariner had the capability to land on the roughest of seas, but this plane also disappeared into the grim silence of the Atlantic. What followed was the greatest search operation in modern maritime history. For five days an armada of 350 planes and twenty-one ships crisscrossed the sea and sky, but no trace of the six aircraft or twenty-six crew members was ever found. To this day it remains a mystery as to what happened. Many believe that the answer to the mystery lies in the UFO phenomenon.

Goodness Gracious, Great Balls of Fire!

On the evening of July 14, a Pan American airliner, flying at an altitude of eight thousand feet, was approaching Norfolk, Virginia, en route to Miami from New York. According to the pilots the night was clear and visibility was unlimited. Just after 8 p.m. Captain William B. Nash and copilot William Fortenberry both sighted a ball of red brilliance in the sky, apparently beyond and to the east of Newport-News. According to the pilots:

> Almost immediately, we perceived six bright objects streaking toward us at tremendous speed. . . . They had the fiery aspect of hot coals, but a much greater glow—perhaps twenty times more brilliant (than the city lights below). . . . Their shape was clearly outlined and evidently circular; the edges were well defined, not phosphorescent or fuzzy. . . . The red-orange color was uniform over the whole surface of each craft.

The single-line formation of double-DC-3 sized UFOs then suddenly seemed to slow its collective speed, with the second and third appearing to overtake the lead light. According to the pilots:

> All together, they flipped on edge, the sides to the left of us going up and the glowing surfaces facing right. . . . They

were much like coins. . . . Then, without an arc or swerve at all, they flipped back together to the flat altitude and darted off in a direction that formed a sharp angle with their first course. . . . The change . . . was acute . . . like a ball ricocheting off a wall.

Captain Nash estimated that the unlighted exposed edges of each craft were about fifteen feet thick and their top surfaces flat. As two additional craft suddenly joined the six, the lights of all eight blinked off, then back on. Remaining in a straight line, the UFOs zoomed westward, climbing in a graceful arc as their lights blinked out . . . one by one. The entire display lasted between fifteen and twenty seconds.

The Nash-Fortenberry sighting (as it came to be known in UFO annals) gained considerable attention quickly throughout the nation, only to be eclipsed five days later by a spectacular sighting over the nation's capitol.

The Day the Earth Stood Still

In 1951 Hollywood released the classic science-fiction thriller, *The Day the Earth Stood Still.* Directed by Robert Wise, the film depicted a humanoid ambassador from an intergalactic organization of planets landing on the lawn of the White House. The alien emissary was named "Klaatu" and he had come to determine if the inhabitants of Earth were worthy of joining the federation or if they needed to be obliterated. Near the end of the film, the alien is murdered (there go our chances at membership in the federation), but is later resurrected aboard his spacecraft. Just one year after the film's release, it appeared that Klaatu might indeed be landing—literally—on the White House lawn!

Around midnight on Saturday, July 19, 1952, a surprised air traffic controller working at the National Airport in Washington, D.C., took note of some bizarre blips on his radar screen. Knowing that no aircraft were flying in the area—just fifteen miles south of the capitol—he quickly informed his immediate supervisor, Harry Barnes. As Barnes recalls:

> Our shift had been on duty about forty minutes. The things which caused fellow air traffic controller Ed Nugent to call me over to the scope were seven pips clustered together irregularly in one corner. We knew immediately that a very strange situation existed. . . . Their movements were completely radical as compared to those of conventional aircraft. They moved with such sudden bursts of intense speed that our radar was unable to track them continuously.

At the same time, some ten miles to the east, Andrews Air Force Base personnel sat stunned as bright orange objects in the southern sky circled, stopped abruptly, and then streaked off at unbelievable speeds. Radar at Andrews picked up the strange phenomenon. Radar screens all over the capitol area were picking up these bizarre blips. This cat-and-mouse game of sighting and radar tracking continued until 3 a.m.

The next evening radar again picked up the presence of UFOs as they performed extraordinary gyrations and reversals. Moving at well over nine hundred miles per hour, the objects gave off a distinct radar echo. Sightings and radar tracking continued off and on during the week and then exploded into a frenzy of activity over the next weekend.

As the the incidents began to intensify in their frequency, and as restricted airspace over the Capitol itself was being violated, the Air Defense Command scrambled a group of F-94s to pursue the radar-mocking UFOs. Visibility over the Washington area was excellent that night. As one of the F-94s moved in on several of the targets, the UFOs simply accelerated out of view.

All through the night, civilian pilots, ground personnel, and radar operators filed continuous reports. Howard Cocklin, the radar controller in the tower at Washington Airport, looked out above the city as the objects rushed back and forth across the night sky. He could see a big orange light right where one of the targets was indicated on his radar. A similar object like an "orange ball of fire trailing a tail" was reported by phone by an airman to Andrews Air Force Base; an officer at the base went outside and saw it too, explaining, "It was unlike anything I had ever seen before." As others watched, the object stopped dead still, and then shot off at an incredible speed and vanished. At one point, three geographically separate radar units locked onto the same target just north of the city. The target suddenly disappeared from all three simultaneously.

As another F-94 approached, the UFOs in unison turned and darted toward the stunned pilot, surrounding his aircraft in seconds. The badly shaken pilot, Lieutenant William Patterson, radioed Andrews AFB to ask if he should open fire. The answer, according to Albert M. Chop, a civilian working as a press spokesman for the Air Force who was present, was "stunned silence. . . . After a tense moment , the UFOs pulled away and left the scene."

The Department of Defense held a rather lively press conference the next morning. Major General John Samford provided the sizzle when he was quoted as saying:

> The objects seem to have unlimited power—that means power of such fantastic higher limits that it is theoretically unlimited—it's not anything we can understand.

Retired Air Force major Donald E. Keyhoe underscored the potential seriousness of this particular UFO encounter by saying:

> Up there in the night sky some kind of super-machines were reconnoitering carefully. From their controlled maneuvers it was plain that they were guided—if not manned—by highly intelligent beings. They might be about to land—the

Capitol would be a logical point for contact. Or they might be about to attack.

In his book entitled *Flying Saucers from Outer Space,* Major Keyhoe points out why it is not surprising that the Capitol was selected by the aliens for this particular close encounter:

UFOs seem to show a great deal of interest in military establishments and in defense areas. There have been numerous sightings over atomic energy plants, Air Force bases, Naval bases, Marine Air Corps stations, aircraft plants, rocket testing bases, and uranium mines.

One of the F-94 pilots who encountered the UFOs that night over Washington was quoted as saying:

We were chasing phantoms. They [the UFOs] not only eluded our best air interceptors but they also escaped any clear definition.

Harry Barnes, one of the air traffic controllers who had supervised radar tracking of the objects said:

There is no other conclusion I can reach but that there were at least ten unidentified flying objects moving above Washington performing gyrations which no known aircraft could perform. There is no other conclusion that I can reach but that for six hours on the morning of July 26 there were at least ten unidentified objects moving above Washington, D.C. They were not ordinary aircraft nor in my opinion could they have been any natural phenomena. No natural phenomena could account for these spots on our radar.

As the Pentagon was being inundated with questions concerning the nocturnal visitation, President Harry Truman asked

Secretary of Defense James Forrester to "find out what in the world—or out of it—is going on!"

Captain C. Pierman, a commercial pilot who was an eye-witness to this congressional close encounter, was quoted as saying:

> In my seventeen years of flying I've seen a lot of falling or shooting stars, but these lights were much faster than anything like that. They were about the same size as the brighter stars, and much higher than my six thousand feet. Please remember that I don't speak of them as flying saucers, only very fast moving lights.

One widely reported news story read as follows:

> WASHINGTON, July 28 (INS)—The Air Force revealed today that jet pilots have been placed on a twenty-four-hour nationwide "alert" against "flying saucers" with orders to "shoot them down" if they refuse to land. It was learned that pilots have gone aloft on several occasions in an effort to shoot the mysterious objects to the ground, but never came close enough to use their guns.

Fifteen years after the incident, the men in the radar rooms at Washington, D.C. told the exact same story to experts from the University of Colorado who had been funded by the government to find an explanation for the UFO phenomenon. The radar technicians were adamant that the sightings over the capitol were quite inexplicable. Today, the Washington incident remains as one of the most unbelievable UFO sightings in recorded history.

It Came from Outer Space

Police officer Lonnie Zamora of Socorro, New Mexico, was in hot pursuit of a speeding vehicle late on the afternoon of April 24, 1964, when all of a sudden a roar filled his ears and he observed a flaming craft descending out of the southwestern sky. Little did Zamora know, but he was about to enter UFO history.

Zamora abandoned his chase and began to head for the site where he had seen the flash of fire. Zamora later said that he expected to find an exploded dynamite shack. Instead, as he made his way through the hilly terrain, he observed a shiny, metallic, car-sized object resting on the ground about 150 yards away. Near the object stood two "people" dressed in what appeared to be white coveralls. They looked like small adults or children. One of them stared at Zamora and appeared to be startled by his presence. Zamora now thought that he might have a car accident on his hands so he radioed the sheriff's office to report a possible automobile accident. As Zamora got out of his car to investigate, he suddenly realized that this was no automobile accident.

The object was between one hundred and two hundred yards away in a gully and it was now in clear sight. It was egg-shaped and was standing on four legs. The craft had a strange insignia on its side, something like an arrow pointing vertically toward a half-circle crown. Zamora briefly lost sight of the craft as he dashed back to his car. Hearing an ominous roar, Zamora glanced back to see the UFO, airborne, heading toward a nearby canyon.

What made this case so solid was the fact that Officer Zamora had a sterling reputation for integrity. In addition, a Project Blue Book team discovered what appeared to be landing marks on the desert ground. In the center of each mark was a burned area that investigators determined was created by the vehicle's exhaust.

J. Allen Hynek, astronomical consultant to Project Blue Book, went to Socorro, New Mexico, aiming to find contradictions to Lonnie Zamora's account. Instead, Dr. Hynek discovered what he termed "one of the soundest, best substantiated cases in UFO history."

No less than the head of Project Blue Book would later tell a CIA audience, "This was the most puzzling UFO case I have ever investigated."

Michigan Madness

In 1965 residents of the state of Michigan witnessed one of the most spectacular waves of UFO sightings in modern history. During the summer months alone there were more than five hundred reported sightings in the Wolverine state. One such case was near Ann Arbor, where fifty people, including twelve police officers in three different counties, observed a glowing object streak across the predawn sky. That same evening, eighty-seven female students at Hillsdale College in Ann Arbor observed an object flying around and flashing bright lights for more than four hours. *Life* magazine chronicled the sightings in one of their summer issues. The opening paragraph of the lead article read as follows:

> Call them what you will—"flying saucers," "unidentified flying objects," or "optical illusions"—they are back again, and they are being seen by more people than ever before. The manifestations this summer almost seem to have reached the proportions of an all-out invasion.

In Washington, D.C., House Representative Gerald Ford of Michigan called for a full congressional investigation into the matter; thus, the first congressional hearing on UFOs began April 5, 1966. The conclusion of the investigation was that something indeed was being seen and that a major university should be given the task of researching the UFO phenomenon further. The University of Colorado was awarded the assignment. Under the direction of physics professor Edward Condon, the University of Colorado research team generated a 1,465-page report on the subject of UFOs (known as the

"Condon Report") at a cost to taxpayers of $500,000.

Police Story

During the dark evening hours of April 17, 1966, Ohio sheriff's deputies Dale Spower and Wilbur Neff had just investigated a traffic accident when they spotted a glowing object hovering above the ground. The pulsating object was about one thousand feet above the ground. As the UFO began to move away, the two officers began pursuing it at speeds exceeding ninety miles per hour. A third officer, Wayne Houston, heard the officers on the radio and joined the chase. Some eighty-five miles later the three officers pulled into a service station to refuel. Officer Frank Panzonella, who had also been chasing the craft, joined up with the trio of officers as they all stood and watched the object hover in the eastern sky. The glowing orb hovered for several minutes and then it shot upward at great speed and disappeared.

Project Blue Book researchers were called in to investigate. The official Air Force report said that at least four experienced police officers (one of them a veteran air crewman) had conducted a two-hour high speed chase of the planet Venus.

Take Me to Your Leader

Anybody can see a UFO. Apparently you just have to be in the right place at the right time. Those who claim to have seen an unidentified flying object include heavyweight boxing champion Mohammed Ali; film star and New Age guru Shirley MacLaine; Beatle John Lennon; the astronomer who discovered the planet Pluto, Dr. Clyde Tombaugh; and the list goes on and on. Perhaps one of the most famous and credible witnesses of all time is former President Jimmy Carter.

On January 6, 1969, while Carter was governor of the state of Georgia he, along with ten members of the Leary, Georgia,

Lions Club, stared in amazement as a bright object appeared in the western sky. President Carter said that the object was

> like a big star, about the same size as the moon, maybe a little smaller. It varied from brighter and larger than a planet to the apparent size of the moon.

In the beginning, the rotating mass of light was stationary in the sky and bluish in color, but as the men watched, the mysterious object began to rush back and forth like a pendulum and it turned a deep red color. Carter commented that the object was "luminous but not solid." Carter had no idea what the object was. The men watched the glowing orb for over ten minutes until it finally began to shrink in size and disappear. Carter did not report the incident until 1973, three years before he was elected President. Some UFO skeptics do not believe that Carter actually saw a flying saucer at all. They believe that Carter saw the planet Venus, which would have been in the same vicinity of the sky on that night. The problem with this skeptical viewpoint is that Jimmy Carter was a trained scientist with a Naval Academy degree in nuclear physics. Carter graduated number one in his senior class and had also served with the U.S. Navy. Surely he could have recognized the planet Venus, which is a common sight in the evening and early morning sky.

When Carter became President in 1976 he pledged to do all he could to get the truth about UFOs out to the American public. Carter was not shy about going on record and expressing his belief in the UFO phenomenon: "I am convinced that UFOs exist. I have personally seen one."

A Sighting for "The Gipper"

In 1974, five passengers aboard a Cessna Citation aircraft saw a UFO. The tiny plane carried pilot Bill Paynter, two security guards, and the governor of California, Ronald Reagan, along with his wife Nancy. As the airplane approached Bakersfield, California, the passengers called Paynter's attention to a strange bright object to the rear of the plane. The object was close, only a couple of hundred yards away. Paynter recalls:

> It was a fairly steady light until it began to accelerate. Then it appeared to elongate. Then the object just took off. It went up at a forty-five–degree angle—at an incredible rate of speed. Everyone in the plane was glued to the sight. The UFO went from normal cruising speed to a fantastic speed instantaneously. If you give an airplane power it will accelerate—but not like a hot rod, and that's what this was like.

A week later Ronald Reagan told the details of this story to Norman Miller, who at the time was the Washington bureau chief for the *Wall Street Journal*. Reagan explained to Miller:

> We watched the object for several hundred miles. It was a bright white light. We followed it to Bakersfield, and all of a sudden to our utter amazement it went straight up into the heavens.

Is it any wonder that later, President Reagan would make more statements concerning UFOs than any other President in history? On eighteen different occasions while in office, Reagan alluded to the subject of unidentified flying objects. One of Reagan's most famous speeches was delivered from the floor of the United Nations where he was quoted as saying:

> I've often wondered what if all of us in the world discovered that we were threatened by an outer power from outer space—from another planet—wouldn't we all of a sudden discover that we didn't have any real differences between us at all?

Mounstrom AFB

On November 7, 1975, an alarm went off at Mounstrom Air Force Base in Montana, the site for launching facilities for the Minute Man missile system. This was no ordinary alert. A special sabotage alert team was immediately dispatched to the area where the alarm was triggered. Once there, the elite strike force came face to face with what was described as a "glowing orange disk about the size of a football field" hovering over the area. As the unit approached, the massive orb began to rise slowly as if in retreat.

Simultaneously, the North American Air Defense Command radar picked up the UFO on its screens. When the object reached an altitude of one thousand feet, Air Force jets were dispatched from Great Falls, Montana, to bring the craft down. However, before the fighters arrived, the object disappeared from the radar screen altogether. The very next day there were more sightings. Each time the jets screamed into the area, the UFOs simply disappeared. The UFO would reappear only after the jets left the scene. Over the next eight months some 130 similar reports were logged at Mounstrom AFB.

Chapter Five

So, What On Earth Is Going On?

Something is being seen, but it isn't known what. . . . By all human standards it hardly seems possible to doubt [UFO existence] any longer.

—Carl Gustav Jung, the Swiss-born founder
of modern psychiatry, *Flying Saucers*

There are two things about the UFO enigma that make it uniquely interesting. The first is that it is probably the deepest mystery that mankind has ever encountered. After fifty years amidst the modern UFO era, the truth about the identity and origin of these objects is shrouded in confusion. Nobody seems to know for sure what is going on here; not the witnesses, not the media, and certainly not the authorities. Ever elusive, ever changing, ever mystifying, the phenomenon of the UFO is indeed a "cosmic chameleon."

The second unique aspect about the UFO phenomenon is that it has been the object of so much denial despite the fact that it is certainly a real phenomenon. Heaven knows we've got more data than we know what to do with! What we lack is a framework.

Confronted with this massive stockpile of evidence that UFOs do in fact really exist, a torrent of questions inevitably flood our mind. How are we to explain it all? How do we as Christians deal with the issue of UFOs? Who are these aliens? Where do they come from? What are they doing here?

Whitley Strieber, writing in the forward of Jacques Vallee's best selling book *Dimensions,* warns us:

> If we come to a correct understanding of the UFO phenomenon, we may well in the process destroy the whole basis of our present beliefs about reality.

J. Allen Hynek, quoted in the *International UFO Journal* agrees with Strieber's assessment when he says:

> When the solution to the UFO puzzle comes, I think it will prove not to be just a step in the march of science but a quantum jump.

Politically Correct

It's been well said that the study of UFOs is much like American politics in one respect: there are only two parties you can join. In politics, you can be only a Democrat or Republican. In Ufology, either you are a debunker who doesn't believe in UFOs at all, or you agree they are spacecraft from another planet. But in reality these are not the only two possibilities. There are really five possible answers for explaining the existence of UFOs. Two of these explanations are natural and three of them are supernatural. Let's look at each one of these possible explanations more closely in an attempt to zero in on exactly "who" or "what" is behind the UFO enigma.

Natural Theory #1

The first natural theory is simply that all UFO sightings are misidentifications of natural phenomena or just plain outright hoaxes. This theory is indeed partially true. As we have already stated, ninety to ninety-five percent of all UFO sightings can be explained away as either misidentifications, hoaxes, or hallucinations. However, this still leaves five to ten percent of UFO/alien encounters that defy any known explanation.

A large majority of the scientific community, which is typically unaware of the observational data except as reported in the popular press, continues to support this natural phenomenon hypothesis. They assert that all the reported sightings can be easily explained away as a combination of observational errors, classical atmospheric phenomenon, and/or man-made objects. This camp has concluded that there is no new knowledge to be gained from further specialized study of reported UFO sightings.

Natural Theory #2

The second natural theory is an evolutionary one. This theory states that just as life supposedly evolved on planet Earth, life has also evolved on other planets as well—some to a point far more advanced than life on our planet. This is the most commonly held theory about the origin of UFOs and the favorite hypothesis of the media at large. Simply stated: UFOs represent visits by extraterrestrials. This theory is commonly referred to as the extraterrestrial hypothesis or ETH.

The question of life beyond Earth (extraterrestrial intelligence) has been debated by scholars, philosophers, and scientists for centuries. The Pythagoreans debated the subject back in the fifth century. Other Greek philosophers speculated about the possibility of life forms inhabiting other worlds. Teng Mu, a scholar of the Sung Dynasty in China, wrote:

> Empty space is like a kingdom, and earth and sky are no more than a single individual person in that kingdom. Upon one tree are many fruits, and in one kingdom there are many people. How unreasonable it would be to suppose that, besides the earth and the sky which we can see, there are no other skies and no other earths.

Those who believe in the extraterrestrial hypothesis would say that we are now experiencing visits from these interplanetary travelers. A majority of the public, as well as the major-

UFO photographed near Albuquerque, New Mexico, June 16, 1963, by Paul Villa

ity of UFO researchers, have supported this hypothesis. Believers in the ETH see UFOs as physical devices controlled by intelligent beings from distant planets who are visiting the Earth as part of a scientific survey, very much in the fashion that we ourselves plan to follow in exploring our own remote planetary environs.

According to ETH proponents, this alien survey of Earth includes the reconnaissance of strategic sites, the gathering of mineral and plant samples, as well as sophisticated interaction with the human and animal life forms present on the planet.

Erich von Daniken, who came to prominence in the 1970s with his bestseller *Chariots of the Gods?*, remains a passionate advocate of the reality of extraterrestrials visiting planet Earth. Von Daniken claims that ancient astronauts have visited and even colonized planet Earth. Von Daniken's theory proposes that our development as a race is the direct result of alien manipulation and experimentation. Von Daniken has become one of the most popular proponents of the ETH theory. Von Daniken himself has stated that his theories came to him while on an astral trip, and that he knows himself to be a reincarnated ancient astronaut.

UFO Cults

It is interesting that there are many world religions that have long preached the existence of extraterrestrial intelligence, and would thus by virtue of their theology be proponents of the ETH. For these individuals, the discovery of extraterrestrial life forms would not be shocking at all. In fact, such a discovery would be expected. The false Japanese religion of Shinto is one example. The holy books of Shinto, the *Kojiki* (*Record of Ancient Things*) and the *Nihongi* (*Records of Japan*), describe in detail the descent of sky gods to marry Earth goddesses. Because of the strong Shinto influence in Japan, it should come as no surprise that UFOs are big business in Japan today, with the Shinto religion itself being a driving force behind the Japanese fascination with UFOs and aliens. The Japanese are intrigued by the possibility that they could discover, through UFO research, certain windows in the atmosphere that could link them back to the realm of the gods.

Nostradamus, the sixteenth-century seer, has a growing family of followers today. Interestingly, Nostradamus drew from space for one of his most intriguing prophecies, saying:

> A great king of terror will descend from the skies,
> The year 1999, seventh month,
> To resuscitate the great king Anglomois,
> Around this time Mars will reign for a good cause.

The religion of Hinduism is another extraterrestrial-friendly religion. One of the primary holy books of Hindu, the *Bhagavad-gita,* makes reference to alien beings from other worlds coming down to Earth. Other notable extraterrestrial-based religions are Buddhism and Mormonism.

The doctrine of the Church of Jesus Christ of Latter-Day Saints is set forth on a series of revelations, including one entitled "The Visions of Moses, as revealed to Joseph Smith the Prophet, in June 1830." This less than inspired revelation tells how Moses "beheld many lands; and each land was called earth, and there were inhabitants on the face thereof." According to Smith's revelation, God instructed Moses that:

> Worlds without number have I created. . . . But only an account of this earth, and the inhabitants thereof, give I unto you. For behold, there are many worlds that have passed away by the word of my power. And there are many worlds that now stand, and innumerable are they to man; but all things are numbered to Me.

Ufologist Jacques Vallee has correctly stated: "If Joseph Smith were alive today he would be considered a contactee."

Mormonism has many links to outer space. James Walker,

himself a former Mormon and now director of the Texas office of the evangelical watchdog organization, Watchman Fellowship, says this about the teaching of Mormonism:

> Mormonism is in a whole different family. . . . Mormonism
> is based on polytheism. Mormons believe God used to be a
> man named Elohim on another planet on a star named
> Kolab and because he was such a good man the other gods
> allowed him to become one of the gods. He lives on this
> planet with his goddess wives having billions of offspring.

The holy books of Buddhism, in their own glittering way, speak of many worlds. One such book is the *Saddharma-Pundarika,* or *Lotus of the True Law.* In this book, the Lord appears before an assembly of "Bodhisattvas," or wise men, "gathered from countless worlds and numbering eight times the grains of sand in the Ganges." He tells them of "many worlds, of golden people, jeweled trees, perfumed winds, wafting showers of petals."

Our Lady of the Flying Disk

In 1917, in what may have been the largest crowd to ever witness a UFO, seventy thousand residents of Fatima, Portugal, gathered in the pouring rain and watched in amazement as the thick gray storm clouds rolled away like the curtains on a stage and a sweet fragrance filled the air. The sun appeared against the clear blue sky as a flat silver disk revolved on its own axis, shooting forth radiant shafts of red, violet, yellow, and blue light in all directions. The huge silver disk was spinning like a windmill and dancing in the sky. Suddenly the disk plunged erratically downward in zigzag fashion, causing thousands of witnesses (believers and unbelievers alike) to fall on their knees in public confession of their sins before the end of the world.

The disk stopped short of ground zero and began slowly rising into the sky in the same irregular fashion before disappearing into the sun, which stood once again fixed in its natural brilliance. The entire display lasted around fifteen minutes.

This amazing sighting was the fifth in a series of sightings that began when three illiterate shepherd children were surprised by a bright flash of light in a nearby pasture (widely known as an old sacred place). Once in the pasture an illuminated figure appeared to the children instructing them to return to the same spot every month. Many ufologists speculate that this famous apparition (commonly referred to as "Our Lady of Fatima") could very well have been an alien spacecraft and the three shepherd children—Lucia, Francisco, and Jacinto—contactees. Was this truly a vision from God? Could it have been a UFO encounter? Or was it some sort of satanic delusion?

After thirteen years of painstaking investigation, the Catholic church offered this report:

> This phenomenon, which no astronomical observatory registered and which therefore was not natural, was witnessed by persons of all categories and of all social classes, believers and unbelievers, journalists of the principal Portuguese newspapers, and even by persons some miles away. Facts which annul any explanation of collective illusion.

The Church of Scientology, Urantia and, of course, the infamous Heaven's Gate, are just a few of the hundreds of extraterrestrial-based religious cults found in the world today.

Weird Science

Today, the search for extraterrestrial intelligence is carried on largely through the use of radio astronomy. Radio astronomy is the science of listening to and studying the characteristics of radio signals generated by both known natural sources as well as unexplained sources in the universe. The first visionary to suggest that ETs might be contacted via radio waves was the renowned inventor and radio pioneer of the 1930s, Nikola Tesla of Colorado. However, it was not until 1959 (the same year that the television show "The Twilight Zone" debuted) that astronomer Frank Drake proposed using a radio telescope to scan the heavens for signs of intelligent life.

The first major attempt at such contact was named Project Ozma and was conducted at the National Radio Astronomy Observatory in Green Bank, West Virginia, under the direction of Dr. Drake. Project Ozma was named "after a land far away, difficult to reach and populated by strange and exotic beings." Drake's objective was to make contact with extraterrestrial intelligence because, according to Drake,

> I find nothing more tantalizing than the thought that radio messages from alien civilizations in space are passing through our offices and homes, right now, like a whisper we can't quite hear.

Drake believed very strongly that contact with ETs would be a very beneficial thing: "Interstellar contact will enrich our lives immeasurably. . . . We will witness the history of the future, not just the past."

According to the now famous "Drake Equation" of the 1960s, there are approximately ten thousand advanced extraterrestrial civilizations in the Milky Way galaxy alone. To make contact with even one, many scientists believe, would be the most monumental event in man's history.

Today, Drakes' dream of "first contact" lives on as massive radio telescope antennas are pointed toward stars that scientists believe are similar to our own sun. The scientists are betting that life would most likely exist on a planet circling a star like our sun.

On October 12, 1992, NASA launched SETI, a ten-year, $100 million search for extraterrestrial intelligence. SETIs sole purpose is to seek the answer to a single question. The $100 million question is: "Is man alone in the universe?"

The SETI (Search for Extraterrestrial Intelligence) project

began at Harvard's Oak Ridge Observatory. It was originally designed to scan sixty-eight percent of the sky. The first multichannel spectrum analyzer used by SETI scanned 131,072 channels. The system was upgraded in 1985 to scan an amazing 8.4 million radio channels. In October 1990, outside of Buenos Aires, Argentina, a second multi-spectrum analyzer was installed. Both machines are part of the SETI network. It is reported that NASA, in coordination with Stanford University, has recently developed a multi-spectrum analyzer capable of listening to a whopping 15 million radio channels. Now, if only ET would just phone home!

The centerpiece to the SETI project is the "Arecibo" radio telescope in Puerto Rico. Arecibo's one thousand-foot-wide antenna dish makes it the largest radio telescope in the world, with the effective power of over 20 trillion watts. This state of the art facility is expertly manned by over one hundred physicists, astronomers, and computer technicians, all poised and staring at control panels in hopes of discovering radio waves that were created by intelligent beings deep in space.

John Billingham, one-time project director of SETI, was quoted as saying:

> The United States wants to be the first nation to make contact. When we make contact it will be the biggest breakthrough in the history of mankind. These advanced civilizations could help us conquer problems like cancer, pollution, food and energy shortages, and natural disasters.

The SETI project is not only trying to receive communication from the ETs, but SETI is also attempting to communicate directly to them. In its attempt to establish two-way communication with the extraterrestrials, SETI armed the *Pioneer 10* and *Pioneer 11* spacecrafts with engraved metal plates, complete with symbols and codes, that are designed to indicate to aliens that find them drifting in space that earthlings are open to communication with the ETs. Also, *Voyager 1* and *Voyager*

2 each carry an elaborate recorded message of words and music for the same purpose. These space probes are even now heading at warp-speed through interstellar space.

Science Fair

Many highly esteemed scientists today hold to the ETH. Let's take a minute to hear from some of these men.

Astrophysicist Alastaire Cameron, in the introduction to his *Anthology of Interstellar Communication,* describes the possibility of life in other worlds as follows:

> This is currently the greatest question in scientific philosophy. Already we are admitting that there may be millions of societies more advanced than ourselves in our galaxy alone. If we can now take the next step and communicate with some of these societies, then we can expect to obtain an enormous enrichment of all phases of our sciences and our arts. Perhaps we shall also receive valuable lessons in the techniques of stable world government.

Scientist Richard Terrile of the Jet Propulsion Laboratory says:

> The time will have to come when we realize that we're not the center of the universe. The galaxy may be teeming with life. There may be billions of civilizations.

Dr. Leo Sprinkle, who himself has interviewed hundreds of UFO witnesses over a period of twenty-five years, is a firm believer in the ETH. Dr. Sprinkle sees modern UFO activity as a part of an overall educational program by ufonauts for humankind on planet Earth. According to Dr. Sprinkle:

> The aliens have placed an embargo on communication with Earth in order to minimize panic. It is possible that we are being slowly introduced to ETs through movies and science fiction, until the evidence of ET visitations becomes more acceptable to the majority of physical scientists.

Bernard Oliver, a distinguished NASA scientist, has stated:

"Many scientists now believe that extraterrestrial life exists, perhaps hundreds or even thousands of civilizations."

Paul Horowitz, past professor of physics at Harvard University, has estimated: "A suitable habitat for life and a mechanism for its origin may exist near many of the billions of stars in our galaxy."

Dr. Hermann Oberth, internationally renowned rocket and space travel authority, and father of the V-1 and V-2 weaponry of World War II, has said:

> These objects [UFOs] are conceived and directed by intelligent beings of a very high order. They probably do not originate in our solar system, perhaps not even in our galaxy.

Dr. Charles Harvard Gibbs-Smith, aeronautical historian at the Victoria and Albert Museum, London, has stated:

> Certainly there are other civilizations, perhaps thousands of times older and wiser. And I believe intelligent beings from these civilizations are visiting us in spacecraft—and have been for years.

Fred Hoyle, in his book *Of Men and Galaxies,* says:

> It is possible that a great intragalactic communications network exists, but that we are like a settler in the wilderness who as yet has no telephone.

Dr. Carl Sagan, Dr. Robert Jastrow, and Dr. Clyde Tombaugh are some other well-known names from the scientific community advocating the extraterrestrial hypothesis. According to Jastrow:

> There are 100 billion stars belonging to the cluster we call our galaxy. Ten billion other galaxies, each with 100 billion stars—and probably a like number of planets—are within the range of the largest telescopes. Perhaps only a

small fraction of them are earthlike planets, but that would mean millions of earthlike planets in our galaxy alone.

Carl Sagan has suggested:

> The most optimistic estimates in the view of many scientists today on the question of how many intelligent civilizations there might be in the galaxy is in the order of one million. This means that only one in every few hundred thousand stars has such a civilization.

George Wald, Noble Prize winner in 1971 for his pioneering work in physiology, has stated: "There could easily be a billion such places in our own galaxy that might just contain life."

Ashley Montague, respected anthropologist, has said:

> When we speak of life beyond the earth, what we mean of course is intelligent life—something resembling life like our noble selves. It is highly probable that there are such other forms of highly intelligent life in the universe and it is probable that many of these life forms are vastly more intelligent than we.

Philip Morrison, author of a book entitled *Possible Modes of Communication with Extraterrestrial Life,* says:

> There are probably thousands, maybe as many as a million inhabitable planets with intelligent life. I believe that there is probably a whole society of these planets. There is not just one. If there was only one we would have no chance of finding it.

University professor Richard Berendzen, who at one time taught a college course entitled "The Search for Intelligent Life in the Universe," has said:

> Each passing year has seen our estimate of the probability

of finding life in space increase along with our capabilities of detecting it. More and more scientists believe that contact with other civilizations is no longer something beyond our dreams but is a natural event in the history of mankind.

Forbidden Science

Some ufologists claim that all extraterrestrials come from the same planet. Others contend that a number of different planets have sent emissaries. Still others postulate that UFOs come from an entirely different period of time altogether—perhaps from the future, sent back to observe their own beginning. Others, like UFO expert Dr. Jacques Vallee, suggest that these extraterrestrials are not extraterrestrial in origin at all, but rather they are beings that come from some fifth or sixth dimension way beyond our comprehension. According to Dr. Vallee in his bestselling book *Dimensions: A Casebook of Alien Contact:*

> We have come to realize that we are dealing with a genuine new phenomenon of immense scope. Although I am among those who believe that UFOs are real physical objects, I do not think they are extraterrestrial in the ordinary sense of the term. In my view they present an exciting challenge to our concept of reality itself. These objects have been seen from time immemorial, and their occupants have always performed similar actions along similar lines of behavior; therefore it is not reasonable to assume that they are simply extraterrestrial visitors. They must be something more. Perhaps they have always been here. On Earth. With us. To put it bluntly, the extraterrestrial theory is not strange enough to explain the facts surrounding UFOs. And I, for one, will be disappointed if UFOs turn out to be nothing more than visitors from another planet.

If they are not spacecraft, what else could UFOs be?

What research framework can account for the physical effects, for their impact on society, for the appearance of their occupants, and for the seemingly absurd dreamlike elements of their behavior? How can we explain that the phenomenon makes itself obvious to rural populations but avoids overt contact, choosing instead to deliver its message in bizarre abductions, in highly strange incidents? My theory goes beyond the notion that these are simply technological vehicles produced by advanced races on another planet.

Instead I believe that the UFO phenomenon represents evidence for other dimensions beyond spacetime; the UFOs may not come from ordinary space, but from a **multiverse** which is all around us, and of which we stubbornly refused to consider the disturbing reality in spite of the evidence available to us for centuries. They could even be fractal beings. The Earth could be their home port. . . .

I believe there is a system around us that transcends time as it [does] space. Others . . . have reached the same conclusion. Some have come away deeply discouraged by the realization best summed up early in this century by Charles Fort in his classic UFO book, *The Book of the Damned:* "We are property." The UFO manifestations cannot be spacecraft in the ordinary nuts-and-bolts sense. The UFOs are physical manifestations that simply cannot be understood apart from their psychic and symbolic reality. What we see here is not an alien invasion. It is a **spiritual** system that acts on humans and uses humans.

If UFOs are indeed somebody else's nuts-and-bolts hardware, then we must still explain how such tangible hardware can change shape before our eyes, vanish in a Cheshire cat manner (not even leaving a grin), seemingly melt away in front of us, or apparently "materialize" mysteriously before us without apparent detection by persons nearby or in neighboring towns. We must wonder, too, where UFOs are hiding when not manifesting themselves to human eyes.

The real question becomes: "Does the extraterrestrial hypothesis explain to our satisfaction the facts of the UFO phenomenon as we know them today?" The answer is a definite and resounding "no." Vallee and many other leading UFO researchers have all but discredited the extraterrestrial hypothesis.

Quantum Leap

Vallee and others argue that one of the main problems with the interplanetary evolution hypothesis is that most scientists, while sympathetic to the belief that life may indeed exist on other planets, are nearly unanimous in their agreement that interstellar travel is outside the realm of possibility. Scientists argue that the tremendous distances involved and the speed required would make such travel next to impossible—regardless of how technologically advanced the life form. No one has ever been able to explain how it is that a spaceship could travel the vast distances that exist between galaxies.

The closest galaxy is some two million light years from Earth. Even if a craft could travel close to the speed of light (186,000 miles per second), it would take a minimum of two million years to make the journey. The nearest star to planet Earth is Alpha Centauri, which is some 4.5 light years (25 trillion miles) away. If a spacecraft could travel one million miles per day it would take seventy thousand years to make the trip.

In yet another scenario, imagine a spaceship carrying ten passengers traveling five light years to and from a nearby star system at seventy percent the speed of light. It is estimated that to make such a journey, a starship would require fuel equal to 500,000 times the amount of energy used in the United States in one year.

In addition to the overwhelming distances involved, one must honestly consider the following facts which argue strongly against intelligent beings from another planet visiting Earth:

Fact #1. Despite claims to the contrary, not one single UFO or alien body has ever been captured. There is not one bolt, screw, chunk of metal, piece of debris, etc. that has ever been found to conclusively prove the existence of an alien spacecraft—much less intelligent alien life.

The British Flying Saucer Review was first published in 1955. Today it is recognized as the leading publication in the world on the subject of UFOs. Over fifty experts worldwide contribute to each issue. An official statement by *BFSR* editor Gordon Creighton is most amazing: "There seems to be no evidence yet that any of these craft or beings originate from outer space."

Fact #2. Despite claims to the contrary, not one UFO has ever crashed on Earth.

Fact #3. There has never been a UFO that has responded to radio signals or any other kind of communication sent from Earth.

Fact #4. No planet has ever been positively identified as the sending station for these UFOs. All messages received to date through psychics, channellers, abductees, etc. have indicated a variety of different planets without any consistent verifiable proof of where these messages originate from.

Fact #5. Science has proven that space is not a vacuum. Space is full of dust, debris, gas, and other particles. There is about one hydrogen atom per cubic centimeter as well as bits of dust and perhaps other material here and there. If a spaceship were traveling at or near the speed of light it would be constantly colliding with this material, producing massive amounts of deadly radiation as intense per square yard as that produced by several hundred atom-smashers. As one scientist put it, "the interplanetary traveler would have a major shielding problem." Nobel Prize winning scientist Professor Edward Buzzel puts it this way: "The speeding space ship would become like an interstellar atom smasher as it hurtled through space."

Fact #6. Physical beings, regardless of their advanced technological state, are still subject to physical laws. In other words, physical beings must operate within the constraints governed by the physical laws of the universe itself. These physical laws would seem to make the prospect of interstellar travel quite implausible. Nobel laureate Professor Edward Purcell of Harvard University has stated: "All this stuff about traveling around the universe in space suits—except for local exploration [within our own solar system] belongs back where it came from, on the cereal box."

Fact #7. As Christians we must rule out life evolving naturalistically on other planets because there are too many problems with the evolutionary theory in general. Most Christians don't believe that life evolved on our own planet—how much less should we believe that life evolved on thousands or millions of other planets. Berkeley-trained scientist and author John Weldon has stated: "You could literally pack the universe with planets so close that no space existed between them, give them perfect conditions for life evolving [based on current theories], and it is still impossible that life would evolve on any of them. The odds are less than one in $10^{100,000,000,000}$, which according to Borel's law is absolute zero."

Fact #8. Another argument against the idea of flying saucers being spacecraft from other planets lies, oddly enough, in the large number of sightings. Research compiled by ufologist Jacques Vallee shows that most sightings are reported to take place at night after 6:00 p.m. with the activity peaking around 10:30 p.m., followed by a secondary predawn peak of activity. Abduction reports show a maximum peak at around midnight. Given such a stable pattern, we are lead to ask: "What would the data look like if most people did not retire early at night?" The answer is simply this—the number of sightings would be significantly higher, the point being that UFO activity, which is nocturnal by nature, is quite high. Also, most landings and sightings occur in sparsely populated areas. What would the sighting count look like if UFOs appeared over densely populated areas? Vallee has estimated from his study that if UFOs are really engaged in a general survey of our planet they must have landed here no fewer than 14 million times in the last forty years. This frequency is totally absurd. According to Vallee:

Using a single probe the size of a beer keg in orbit a thousand miles above the Earth, human technology as it exists today would be able to capture in a few weeks most of the important facts about the planet's geography, weather, vegetation, and culture. Given the Earth's abundant emission of radio and television programs for the last fifty years, even the deployment of such a space probe might be unnecessary.

This is one of the little recognized facts about the UFO problem that any theory has yet to explain. The theory of random visitation does not explain it. Either the UFOs select their witnesses for psychological and sociological reasons, or they are something entirely different from space vehicles. In either case, their appearances are staged!

Erich Von Daniken (the former Swiss hotel manager, bartender, and waiter-turned-Ufologist and author) has this to say about the alien learning curve:

For thirty years at least, there have been accounts of visitations and even abductions, yet the manner and form of the aliens' investigations into us have never altered. The victims are always treated according to a fixed routine. No medical research team on Earth would need to examine so many thousands of people like this. By the hundredth patient, at the most, they would have the information they needed.

Dr. Alan Hynek has stated:

> I have come to support less and less the idea that UFOs are nuts-and-bolts' spacecraft from other worlds. There are just too many things going against this theory. To me, it seems absolutely ridiculous that super intelligent beings would travel millions of light years to do relatively stupid things like stop cars, collect soil samples, and frighten people. I think we must re-examine the evidence. We must begin to look closer to home.

The bottom line is that close encounters are far more numerous than required for any physical survey of the Earth. It is difficult to believe that advanced space explorers would need to land on the surface of a planet to analyze its soil, take samples of the flora and fauna, and produce a complete map of the surface. If these beings are so intellectually advanced, why is it taking them so long to survey this planet and its inhabitants?

Fact #9. UFOs have been seen throughout history and have consistently received or provided their own explanation within the framework of each culture. In antiquity UFO occupants were regarded as gods; in the ninth century UFOs were seen in the form of vessels in the sky; in medieval times UFOs were seen as magicians or dragons; in the nineteenth century, as scientific geniuses; in our own time, as interplanetary travelers. The UFO phenomenon seems to remain consistently one step ahead of human technology. If these objects have been seen from time immemorial, and if their occupants have always performed similar actions along similar lines of behavior, then it is not reasonable to assume that they are "simply" extraterrestrial visitors. They must be something more. The existence of the UFO phenomenon throughout recorded human history demonstrates that UFOs are not a contemporary phenomenon. One author makes this observation:

A historical survey reveals that reports of strange objects in the sky are laced through documents of the ancient and recent past. Interestingly, the records seem to indicate that UFOs have adapted themselves to the cultural milieu and the technological capacities of the observers.

Jacques Vallee agrees with this observation:

UFOs are paranormal in nature and a modern space age manifestation of phenomenon that assumes different guises in different historical contexts.

In his book *Passport to Magonia,* Dr. Vallee provides the following historical perspective on UFO sightings:

I think we need to journey well beyond the specific frame of reference involving UFOs and probe the larger mechanism that generates religious visions, mystical raptures, appearances by supernatural creatures, and flying saucers— all rely on the same processes and mechanisms, all sharing similar characteristics and effects on the human observer, depending on the predominate belief structure of the given culture. Ezekiel saw a burning wheel. In the Middle Ages angels, dragons, and fiery crosses appeared in the sky, and a legendary celestial region called Magonia was said to be inhabited by extraordinary beings who traveled in aerial ships, sometimes descending to abduct unsuspecting humans. In nineteenth century America, people saw airships

resembling zepplins. Since 1947 we have seen flying saucers.

In his book *Transformation,* abductee Whitley Strieber makes
the same historical connection:

> The visitor experience is old. Two hundred years ago a
> farmer might have come in from his plowing and said, "I
> saw fairies in the glen." A thousand years ago he might
> have seen angels flying. Two thousand years ago it would
> have been Dionysus leaping in the fields. Four thousand
> years ago he might have seen the goddess Earth herself
> walking those old hills, her starry robe sparkling with the
> pure light of magic. . . . We hide from the visitors. We hide
> in beliefs. They're the gods. They're gentry, dwarfs, elves.
> They're demons or angels. Aliens. The unconscious. The
> oversoul. Hallucinations. Mass hysteria. Lies. You name it.
> But what they never are, what we never allow ourselves to
> face, is the truth.

Fact #10. Another fact which argues strongly against
the extraterrestrial hypothesis is the super physics of
the UFOs. Levitation, extreme acceleration and decel-
eration, right-angle turns while traveling at thousands
of miles per hour, absence of sonic booms, surrounding
clouds, colored halos, dazzling brightness, luminous
trails, lingering clouds, pungent odors, baked earth,
charred organic matter, humming sounds, and the phenomenal ability to materialize and dematerialize are just
a few of the standard features found on todays UFOs.

The apparent ability of UFOs to manipulate space and time
suggests radically different and richer alternatives for their
identity. In most cases of UFO sightings the spacecraft does
not disappear by moving away, even at high speed. It simply
vanishes on the spot, or it slowly fades away, sometimes leaving a whitish cloud, sometimes also producing the sound of

an explosion. There are quite a few reported cases where two distinctly different UFOs hovering in clear sky will converge and eventually merge into one singular object. In some cases UFOs are reported to enter directly into the ground. Reliable photographs and video tape clearly show UFOs materializing and dematerializing. This type of behavior is totally in contradiction to what physical objects are able to do. UFOs consistently violate the laws of motion and physics as we know them. Even our most sophisticated aircraft cannot come close to duplicating the maneuvers of these alien craft. Physicist James McCampbell has stated:

> Evidence left at landing sites leaves little room for doubt that UFOs are heavy, ponderous objects when at rest. Yet in flight, their startling departures, sudden stops, and right angle turns at high speed require them to be virtually massless.

Most UFO sightings are not even of an object or a craft; they are reports of lights—massive, multicolored, intense, pulsating, hypnotic lights that are accompanied by strange sounds. In other words, UFOs don't always behave like material objects ought to behave.

My Stars! Where in the World?

Fact #11. Yet another reason the ETH has fallen on hard times is the mixed signals given by the aliens themselves as to their planet of origin. Dan Ackroyd's extraterrestrial nuclear family, the former "Saturday Night Live" Coneheads, used to say they were from "France" when pressed about their origins. "Zeta Reticuli," in the southern constellation of Reticulus, was the location given to Betty and Barney Hill by their abductors. In 1897 an alien airship was sighted and its occupants invited witnesses to come with them to "a place where it never rains." On another occasion, aliens explained to startled witnesses that "we're from anywhere, but we shall be in Greece tomorrow!"

On July 23, 1947, near Pitanga, Brazil, a group of surveyors saw a disk-shaped craft land near them. Three beings in shiny clothes and translucent suits emerged from the craft and drew a solar system map for the benefit of the witnesses and pointed to Uranus as if to indicate they came from there.

Another group of aliens claimed to be from "Clarion," an alleged planet in our own solar system going the same speed as the Earth but constantly hidden from us by the sun. Other ufonauts claimed to hail from the constellation Orion, still others from another world called Lanulos. Psychic Jeanne Dixon has stated that UFOs are flown by women pilots and that they come from a planet beyond Jupiter that remains undiscovered.

A complex series of messages allegedly coming from the "Cosmic Federation of Planets" has been received by UFO channelers in Spain and France. These messages are said to originate from space brothers from "Ummo," a planet that rotates around the star "Iumma," recorded on Earth's star charts under the designation "Wolf 424." Psychic and UFO student Uri Geller claims that his psychic powers come to him from a form of consciousness emanating from the planet "Hoova."

The Pleiades, Titan, Alpha Centauri, Andromeda, Arcturus, Iarga, Capella, Korender, Tau Ceti, Epsilon Eridani, Draco, Lyra, Selo, and Sirius are just a few of the thousands of forwarding addresses given by alien visitors.

ETH R.I.P.

Based on the previously listed eleven facts, it is becoming more and more evident that no extraterrestrial hypothesis is credible. UFOs cannot be adequately explained within a natural context. Therefore, UFOs must be interpreted in a supernatural or spiritual context. An increasing number of scientists and ufologists alike are coming over to this type of thinking. Even avowed agnostic John Keel, a leading ufologist, has said:

> The only hypothesis that can answer all of the questions posed by all of the sightings is the paraphysical or spiritual hypothesis.

Another leading scientist and UFO researcher has stated:

> The extraterrestrial theory draws conclusions of a profoundly "spiritual" nature, while conveniently avoiding the controversial label. Entities that operate with a total disregard for the inviolate laws of physics traveling at the speed of light or faster and having solved "all their problems" would have to be classified as "spiritual," semantic arguments notwithstanding.

John Keel, one of the most respected researchers in the UFO field, has noted:

> Over and over again, witnesses have told me in hushed tones, "You know, I don't think that thing I saw was mechanical at all. I got the distinct impression that it was alive."

Dr. Jacques Vallee sums up the frustration felt by many UFO researchers when he says:

> Why is it, I wondered, that the occupants of UFOs behave so much like the denizens of fairy tales and elves of ancient folklore? Why is the picture we can form of their world so much closer to the medieval concept of Magonia, the magical land above the clouds, than to a description of an extraterrestrial planetary environment? And why are UFOs becoming a new religious form?

In his book *Angels: An Endangered Species,* author Malcolm Godwin points out a passel of parallels between angels and aliens.

Both exist in inner and outer space and are superior beings by virtue of being closer to Deity; they tend to be miraculously gifted in languages, speaking in the tongue of whatever land they visit; they are literally "messengers"; both use disks, wheels, or saucers as transportation; both are beings of light and radiate subtle auras; both convey serious concern over the welfare of the people of our planet. Witness and witnessed seem cosmically bound together with a sense of oneness.

Even the famous evangelist Billy Graham has said: "UFOs are astonishingly angel-like in some of their reported appearances."

So what about the supernatural explanations? The supernatural possibilities are where we really begin to discover sensible biblical explanations for the UFO phenomenon. There are basically three supernatural explanations available to us.

Supernatural Theory #1

First, God could have created intelligent life on other planets—and one or more of these technologically advanced life forms is now visiting us here on planet Earth. Although this option is possible, it hardly seems to make any sense. Why would these life forms want to come to Earth? Would the life form be fallen or unfallen? Why would God allow them to come here? What would the purpose of their visit be? Although the Bible clearly says that God created the heavens and the Earth, the Bible makes no mention of God creating life on any of these other planets.

Supernatural Theories 2 & 3

The second and third supernatural explanations argue that UFO phenomenon are angelic manifestations (the good angels) or demonic manifestations (the fallen angels). Based on the antibiblical messages typically received by people who claim to be in contact with UFOs (more on this later) and the evil things alien entities are reported to do, we can quickly rule out that these are God's holy angels. This leaves us with only one viable explanation for the UFO phenomenon and that is that they are indeed fallen angels. It is our belief that the UFO enigma is a **demonically driven phenomenon**. In our research of this subject, there is nothing in the realm of ufology that we don't find explained by the realm of the demonic. There is a consistent parallel between UFOs and the demonic/satanic that cannot be denied. There is a clear parallel between UFOs and the occult, as well as UFOs and the New Age movement.

The Devil You Say?

But why would demonic beings want to manifest themselves in this way? Why would demons want to masquerade as ET? Christian ufologist John Weldon provides us with some insight on this question:

> The spiritual forces behind the world of the occult tailor themselves to different cultures and different people's expectations and world views. At first glance, who would think that demons might be behind something like UFOs? But we live in an age where people are talking more and more about life on other planets, where we've been to the moon, and where we're very interested in exploring our solar system in search for intelligent life. In this space age, it is actually more logical that demonic entities would use something like UFOs in order to get across their anti-biblical, anti-Christian messages. When people become fascinated by this realm, then they get more and more involved, and they may end up in what is called contacteeism, or direct occult contact with alleged aliens. This is where people end up getting possessed, where they get taken over by these entities, and receive messages through them. I estimate conservatively that millions of people around the world believe these messages. It's just one more form of spiritual decep-

tion. And something like this is actually expected when you consider the occult from a Christian perspective.

Weldon goes on to explain that the demonic hypothesis isn't just a "Christian theory." According to Weldon:

There have been a number of secular researchers, even atheistic researchers, who have said, if you look at the demonological tradition throughout history, this is what we find in the realm of the UFOs. These are first-class UFO researchers like Dr. Jacques Vallee, John Keel, and many others. So the demonic theory should be taken seriously by people who are wondering what UFOs really are and not dismissed out of hand as merely an idea developed by some Christians who are uncomfortable with the idea of alien life. The truth is that most people have no idea what UFOs are. They either assume they're extraterrestrials or hoaxes, but they really don't know; they're baffled by it. Significantly the demonic theory offers the highest level of explanatory power of any theory.

John White, author of *Aliens Among Us,* puts it like this:

The aliens always approach us under cover of dark. They never say exactly why they are abducting us. The whole thing seems suspicious to me, like a Trojan horse; and I have to express my concern about what is going on. If the aliens change their ways; if they come in broad daylight and come clean about their good intentions, then I'll be happy to welcome them into human society. If they do not, I'll continue to regard them as sly, thieving, underworld creatures whose disposition is evil, even if they disguise themselves as good. And whether they turn out to be physical, paraphysical, or metaphysical in nature, has no bearing on this conclusion.

Secular ufologist Brad Steiger echoes the same thought:

I cannot help questioning whether the space brothers might not be angels, spirits, or other messengers hiding themselves in more contemporary and thereby more acceptable, personae.

UFO author and abductee Whitely Strieber describes how the aliens made him feel:

I felt an absolutely indescribable sense of menace. It was hell on Earth to be there, yet I could not move, couldn't cry out, couldn't get away. I lay as still as death, suffering inner agonies. I thought I was going to suffocate. My throat was closed, my eyes swimming with tears. The sense of being infested was powerful and awful. I could smell them and it was a nauseating odor—it smelled like sulfur.

To this day, Strieber wrestles with fears that his visitors were evil:

They were predators and they were going to eat my soul; they were demons and they were going to drag me off to hell; they were vicious aliens and they were going to steal us all for some kind of experiment. Mostly they terrified me. One does not want to develop a relationship with a hungry panther.

Christian author Dave Hunt, author of over eighteen books, says this concerning the nature of the alien visitors: "I believe they are demonic. I believe all of the evidence clearly indicates this."

In his best-selling book *Confrontations,* ufologist Jacques Vallee comes to the conclusion that there is a lot more evidence that alien beings are evil than there is that they are good. During his research for *Confrontations,* Vallee investigated over one hundred UFO events from around the globe. According to Vallee:

Many of them involved secondary physical and medical effects, including twelve cases of fatal injuries in which the victim typically survived less than twenty-four hours.

The late American scientist Dr. J. Allen Hynek, perhaps the most widely respected UFO researcher to date, never used the word "demon," but Dr. Hynek completely rejected the hypothesis that UFO/alien encounters were extraterrestrial in their origin. According to Dr. Hynek:

> The UFO phenomenon, in its totality, is surprisingly complex. The man on the street's simple opinion that either UFOs are all nonsense or that visitors from outer space do exist is brutally destroyed by close study. Deeper acquaintance reveals a subject that has not only potentially important scientific aspects, but sociological, psychological, and even *theological* aspects as well.

Hynek also submitted: "UFOs are part of some parallel reality, slipping in and out of sequence with our own." This was a hypothesis that obviously pained Hynek as an empirical scientist. Yet after thirty years of interviewing witnesses and investigating sighting reports, radar contacts, and physical traces of saucer landings, no other hypothesis seemed to make sense to him.

One commentator has written:

> Aside from all the conjectured prohibitions against the likelihood of contact with unfallen extraterrestrials, the fact is that the actual cases of reported contact suggest that they are anything but unfallen. Abduction, psychological and psychic manipulation and violence, sexual assault, and physical attack are not uncommon features of UFO contact.

John Keel, another of the growing number of ufologists who have abandoned the extraterrestrial hypothesis, has concluded that the flying saucers are but one thread in a much larger thematic quilt:

> The real UFO story must encompass all of the many manifestations being observed. It is a story of ghosts and phantoms and strange mental aberrations; of an invisible world which surrounds us and occasionally engulfs us; of prophets and prophecies, and gods and demons. It is a world of illusion and hallucination where the unreal seems very real, and where reality itself is distorted by strange forces which can seemingly manipulate space, time, and physical matter—forces which are almost entirely beyond our powers of comprehension.

Keel goes on to add:

> Obviously there is some kind of intelligence behind all of these manifestations. It is very mischievous, with a great sense of humor. Would beings from some distant galaxy travel hundreds of light years to play such tricks on us? . . . In my own peculiar adventures with people claiming to be in contact with the UFO entities, I found that the representatives of that superior technology in the sky were astonishingly stupid, had a wild, even vicious sense of humor, and also had furious tempers like the devils, demons, and Valkyries of old. . . . If the source is crazy for teasing us so pointlessly, what are we who allow ourselves to be so easily teased?

In 1969 the United States Air Force commissioned Dr. E. U. Condon of the University of Colorado to conduct a study of the UFO phenomenon. The result of this study was the famous Condon Report. Although this report has been harshly criticized and ridiculed by many ufologists as just another example of a government cover-up, the report did arrive at some most interesting conclusions.

First, the Condon Report flatly rejected the idea that the

Earth was being visited by aliens from distant planets. According to the Condon Report, there was no hard evidence that UFO spaceships were from extraterrestrial civilizations. However, the report did confirm that the objects that were being sighted were indeed real. According to report findings, the objects seen were just as material as any other physical objects, although maybe only temporarily so. However, the sightings of UFOs, spaceships, and other alien aircraft, as well as their occupants, should be attributed to paraphysical phenomena. In other words, according to the Condon Report, UFOs belong in the same category as seances, spiritist movements, etc. Once again the UFO phenomena is categorized within a supernatural/spiritual framework.

Veteran UFO researcher John Weldon says:

> How credible is it to think that literally thousands of extraterrestrials would fly millions of light years simply to teach New Age philosophy, deny Christianity, and support the occult? And why would the entities actually possess and inhabit people just like demons do if they were really advanced extraterrestrials?

The French National Council for Scientific Research issued the following statement on the demonic nature of the UFO phenomenon:

> UFO behavior is more akin to magic than to physics as we know it, and modern ufonauts and the demons from past ages are probably identical.

It is interesting that the word "demon" in the Greek comes from the root word for "knowledge" or "intelligence," implying that the demons have access to knowledge and information denied to ordinary mortals. Could it be that demons are using their superior knowledge to deceive us into welcoming them as interplanetary travelers?

Abductee Whitley Strieber isn't taking any chances:

After my experience that I describe in my book *Communion,* I thought that it might be a good idea to accept the idea of the devil, just in case that is what I saw. If you look closely at the life of the world, you see very clearly the workings of evil in the world. There seems to be a sort of machinery behind it that is far beyond just the accident of human life.

Like Strieber, thousands of other people have also sensed something evil and demonic within the UFO enigma. Behind the UFO phenomenon, something is definitely there probing people, inspecting people, planting thoughts in their minds, and manipulating their bodies.

Amazingly, agnostic John Keel, a world renowned expert on UFOs and author of many books, sees the parallels between demons and UFOs. According to Keel:

Thousands of books have been written on the subject of demonology, which is the ancient and scholarly study of monsters and demons. The manifestations and occurrences described in this literature are exactly identical to the UFO phenomenon. Victims of demonic possession suffer from the same medical and emotional symptoms as the UFO contactees.

Who can forget the scene in Steven Spielberg's film *Close Encounters of the Third Kind* where a UFO emerges from the midnight sky near a rural farm house. As the UFO descends near the house, there is a corresponding outbreak of strange, bizarre, poltergeist-like activity that begins to take place. Toys begin running around all over the house, screws begin unscrewing, cabinet doors begin opening and shutting wildly, lights begin turning on and off. The entire house seems to be possessed. The clear message of this frightening scene is simply this: The same people who run haunted houses are running the UFO business as well. It is interesting to note that at the time of the filming of *Close Encounters,* French Ufologist

Jacques Vallee (Vallee is depicted in the film by the French scientist Lacombe) objected strenuously to the portrayal of alien beings as "benign brothers" from another world. Vallee, who served as a consultant for the project, was overruled by the producers of the film who were more interested in box office appeal than in accurately depicting the nature of the alien beings.

Arthur C. Clarke, one of the most influential science fiction writers of our time, also hinted at the possible demonic nature of our alien visitors. Clarke is the author of *2001: A Space Odyssey* and *2010*, as well as the host of the syndicated television series "Arthur Clarke's Strange Universe." In the sci-fi classic *Childhood's End*, Clarke depicts the last generation of man seeing its offspring transformed into something totally nonhuman, but superior to humans. Authors Woodrow Nichols and Brooks Alexander comment on Clarke's influence and the link to the demonic:

> It is probably not too much to say that [*Childhood's End*] became the cornerstone for the developing world view of a whole generation. In the book itself, UFOs arrive on Earth at a critical stage in the international arms/space race to save us from nuclear holocaust. The ships are crewed by "the Overlords," a race with massive intellects, but a curious reluctance to show themselves to the earthlings whom they proceed to rule with a dictatorship that is orderly as well as truly benevolent. After a long duration, they reveal themselves, and lo! they look like devils. But no . . . they are actually high-minded guardians, watching over mankind on behalf of the mysterious "Overmind," as it prepares to guide us through enormous and inconceivable evolutionary transformations.

In 1969 the United States Printing Office issued a 4,000-page document entitled *UFOs and Related Subjects: An Annotated Bibliography.* The compiler of this massive work was the senior bibliographer for the Library of Congress, Ms. Lynn Catoe. During her research, Ms. Catoe read over sixteen hundred books and related articles on the subject of UFOs. Catoe's massive bibliography was compiled at the request of the United States Air Force and is currently on file in the Library of Congress. In the preface to her bibliography, Ms. Catoe makes a most startling statement:

> A large part of the available UFO literature is closely linked with mysticism and the metaphysical. It deals with subjects like mental telepathy, automatic writing, and invisible entities, as well as phenomena like poltergeist manifestations and possession. . . . Many of the UFO reports now being published in the popular press recount alleged incidents that are strikingly similar to demonic possession and psychic phenomena which have long been known to theologians and parapsychologists.

French ufologist Dr. Jacques Vallee, who has addressed the United Nations on the subject of UFOs and authored eight books on UFOs, sees a clear connection between the UFO phenomenon and the spiritual realm of the demonic. Dr. Vallee is recognized as the world's premier scientist in the realm of investigating UFOs. In his book *Messengers of Deception,* Vallee makes this most amazing statement: "An impressive parallel exists between UFO occupants and the popular conception of demons."

In his book *Confrontations,* Vallee points out:

> The medical examinations of which UFO abductees are said to be subjected to are often accompanied by sadistic sexual manipulation reminiscent of the medieval tales of encounters with demons. . . . I believe that when we speak of UFOs as being instances of space visitations, we are looking at the phenomenon on the wrong level. We are not dealing with successive waves of visitation; we are dealing with a

control system. UFOs are the means through which man's concepts are being rearranged. They [the powers behind UFOs] are engaging in a worldwide enterprise of subliminal seduction.

Dr. Vallee as an agnostic comes to basically the same conclusions that we do as Christians. Vallee says that UFOs are real, but they are not physical. According to Vallee, they are "messengers of deception." Vallee's conclusions are based on his twenty-five years of research. These entities, according to Vallee, seem to be preparing mankind psychologically for some ultimate delusion that's too horrible to even imagine as yet.

It seems that more and more UFO investigators like Vallee, Keel, Steiger, Weldon, Catoe, Strieber, and Hynek have moved away from the extraterrestrial hypothesis and toward embracing the possibility that UFO and contactee phenomenon are directly related to demonology—that the aliens may in reality be fallen angels.

The Gospel According to ET

On a recent Worldwide Web "surfing safari," I came across the following Web site:

Alien Message to Humanity

Since the times of ancient Egypt it has been recorded that extraterrestrial life has been in frequent contact with the human race. Extraterrestrial life has been covered up by various organizations around the world. Now is your chance to

WITNESS THE TRUTH!!!!

Hear an authentic live message from an alien being directed to all of humanity and you will not believe what you are about to hear! Hear the message that is creating shockwaves of controversy all over the world! **Please call now!!**

This may be the most important call of your life!

Dial 1-900 - __ __ __ __ __ __ __

To my disappointment, the number had been disconnected. Apparently ET was having difficulty paying his phone bill. Whatever the case, ufonauts seem to be communicating with earthlings in an ever-increasing frequency. The content of these messages is most fascinating, especially as one places them within the framework of the demonic.

One of the main reasons Christian UFO researchers are embracing the demonic hypothesis is because as UFO contactees "channel" messages from "space brothers," certain consistent themes keep appearing: a belief that mankind's evolution is manipulated by a higher civilization; a hope that our inability to achieve social peace would be answered by help from above; a blending of expectation of alien contact with goals of planetary unification and the elimination of the money system; an overlap of the UFO phenomenon with New Age spirituality; and an acceptance of "alien" teachings not through reason, but through an irrational leap of faith. More and more the mountain of evidence places UFO activity not within an extraterrestrial framework, but rather within a spiritual and religious framework. Most UFO contactees describe their encounters with "extraterrestrials" in terms more in line with occult mysticism, telepathic communication, and psychic manifestations. In fact, the religious undertones of UFO contacts have been so strong that many UFO religious cults have arisen. Let's take a closer look at some of these "space messages" in an attempt to determine their true origin:

We come from the Interplanetary Confederation of Solar Systems and our purpose and mission is to aid our brother man on the planet Earth as the new age dawns. The teacher that was known to you as Jesus was able to use many more of the abilities than the people of this planet. Man, upon planet Earth, has misinterpreted the meaning of this man's life. He was no different than any of you. He was simply able to remember certain principles which may be realized by any one at any time. It is only necessary that you avail yourselves to our contact thru meditation and begin to realize that which is rightfully yours—the truth of the creation and the truth of your position in it.

Know ye not that ye are gods? We have been puzzled at times by the inability of the people in general on this planet to be awakened to this simple truth. We find that the state of hypnosis brought about by the the the evolution of thought of the people of this planet is so great that it is necessary for man to maintain a constant awareness of his spiritual nature through the process of meditation.

Man is now in a transitional period before the dawn of a new age. Peace, love, brotherhood, and understanding are man's part. Man will witness the dawning of a great new era very soon.

You are like children playing with terrible and dangerous toys which will destroy you. We can do nothing! A cosmic law says that each world must make its own path—to survive or to perish. You have chosen the second. You are destroying your planet. . . . As your elder brothers in this cosmos, we urgently desire with all our hearts your salvation. Do not destroy your beautiful blue planet, a rare atmospheric world that floats so majestically in space full of life. It is your choice.

Your science is developing according to a misguided, casual principle. Because of your false view of knowledge, you are developing an erroneous kind of consciousness—one that is trivial and egocentric, concerned only with yourselves as the center of the universe.

Human beings are not ready to communicate with us and

accept our existence. If we showed ourselves openly, you would act aggressively and consider us as enemies. Your current behavior does not allow us to appear before you— you would be seized by panic. Your consciousness is so riddled with religious and scientific misconceptions that it would not be possible for us to approach you openly.

If man does not raise his vibratory rate within a set period of time, severe Earth changes and major cataclysms will take place. Such disasters shall not end the world, but shall serve as cataclysmic crucibles to burn off the dross of unreceptive humanity. Those who die in such dreadful purgings will be allowed to reincarnate on higher levels of development so that their salvation will be more readily accomplished.

Man is on the brink of tremendous changes and breakthroughs.

People of Earth, you are becoming fourth dimensional [meaning that your humanity is evolving into a new species] whether you are ready or not. Leave the old to those who cling to the old. Don't let the New Age leave you behind.

We are concerned with earthly government's deliberate determination to extinguish humanity and turn this planet into a cinder. Our missions are peaceful, but this condition occurred before in the solar system and the planet Lucifer was torn to bits. We are determined that this shall not happen again.

Prepare yourselves, for the day now closely approaches and those who are not so prepared must vanish from the face of this Earth. Those who align themselves with the things of the Old must surely be destroyed with the age of decay and darkness.

The soul Satan, Lucifer, and Jaweh, who had many other names, has factually been overcome, has seen the error of his ways and actions and has joined the forces of light, truth, and good. Satan has given up, he has exchanged his strong ego and erroneous beliefs for truth, and now is a servant or server of the light! So fear no longer this evil-doer! He no longer does evil works but rather, he channels light—clear and pure and has become a Way Shower!

In his book *Flying Saucer Pilgrimage,* author Bryant Reeves makes the following observation concerning the content of these messages:

From our analysis, the teachings of the space beings appear to support many of the principles taught in Oriental philosophy—by seers of the Far East.

Popular New Age/UFO author Brad Steiger has been following these messages from alleged aliens for decades. Steiger believes that these messages are so important that he has included many of them in a book entitled *The Fellowship,* which is part of his attempt to codify these messages into a new bible of sorts. According to Steiger:

Although these paraphysical, multidimensional gods have always co-existed with us, in the last thirty years they have been accelerating their interaction with us in preparation for a fast-approaching time of transition and transformation. This period, we have been told, will be a difficult one; and for generations our prophets and revelators have been referring to it as the Great Cleansing, Judgment Day, Armageddon. But we have been promised that, after a season of cataclysmic changes upon the Earth plane, a New Age consciousness will infuse the planet. It is to this end that the gods have been utilizing the UFO as a transformative symbol.

It should be clear to any discerning Christian that these messages are coming straight from the "master of deception" himself—Satan. The gospel according to ET finds its origin in seducing spirits who are spreading their demonic doctrines in an attempt to deceive the world prior to the return of Christ.

Chapter Six

Invasion of the Body Snatchers

Although no one can prove that people are actually taken aboard UFOs, if you should find yourself in this predicament, try to remain calm. Observe and remember as much as you can; even ask questions. Try to grab something and bring it back with you as evidence of your experience. As in life, having a sense of humor, and using your intelligence will help you deal with this most unusual situation.

—Ufologist Brian A. Borashas

UFO Mania

As we have said, the modern UFO era began over fifty years ago on June 24, 1947, with pilot Kenneth Arnold's sighting of nine UFOs flying along the mountain tops in Washington State. Since then, thousands of UFOs have been reported, but most of the sightings have turned out to be sightings of the planet Venus, weather balloons, hallucinations, or hoaxes. However, the evidence supporting the existence of UFOs is so vast that no intelligent human being can look at the data systematically and say, "Nothing is there." Make no mistake about it—today in the United States there is a widespread belief in UFOs. At least one of every two Americans believe in the existence of UFOs.

But belief in UFOs is not just an American phenomenon. Today, UFOs are a global phenomenon. UFOs have appeared in every country. Forty-five percent of the enlightened youth of France believe in UFOs. In Yokohama, Japan, a large white saucer dominates a hillside park. Crudely painted UFOs adorn the tin shacks of the barrios of Rio de Janeiro. In Brazil, a hot spot of UFO activity, two-thirds of the population has come to believe that UFOs are real. In Belgium during 1990 there were more than twenty-six hundred sightings of a triangular UFO. There are literally hundreds of millions of people around the world who believe that UFOs are real.

Beyond Bizarre

Over the past twenty years, beliefs about UFOs have become more and more bizarre. Ideas no one would have taken seriously in the past are mainstream today. The latest trend within ufology is the proliferation, over the last forty years, of alien abduction cases. For most people, abduction images come from B-movies, science fiction books, or cartoons. However, in the last several years even the bizarre subject of alien kidnappings has gone mainstream. Since 1961 (the Barney and Betty Hill case), thousands of people have been coming forward with unbelievable tales of extraterrestrial kidnappings—alien abductions.

According to a recent analysis of the 1991 Roper Organization poll on "Unusual Personal Experiences," one in fifty Americans—approximately five million people are "probably" abductees. One by-product of this abduction trend is the proliferation over the last ten years of abduction-based books and movies, such as Whitley Strieber's *Communion,* Budd Hopkin's *Intruders,* Travis Walton's story, *Fire in the Sky,* and Dr. John Mack's *Abduction.*

In his book *UFOs: A Manual for the Millennium,* author and UFO researcher Phil Cousineau writes this concerning the abduction phenomenon:

> On June 29, 1987, the abduction phenomenon made the pages of the venerable *Washington Post* with a curious tug-and-pull headline: "Secrets in the Saucers: Unidentified Facts Fly at AU Symposium." Their story covered the Mutual UFO Network (MUFON) Eighteenth Annual International Symposium on Unidentified Aerial Phenomena at the American University. Presumably, the "secret" was that a few hearty souls came forth at the convention to reveal what had been transpiring "inside" those legendary saucers these past forty years.
>
> "It was the first abduction that we know of," Shirley A. Coyne, a Michigan housewife with two children and three grandchildren, told the crowd of 450 folks. "I was taken from my bed by two little beings who were two and a half, three feet tall. They came into my bedroom, took me through the living room. . . . It was like we were floating, not walking. I had no control. They took me aboard this craft and gave me an examination . . . very painful. They did all kinds

Betty and Barney Hill, who believed they were abducted and taken aboard a UFO in September 1961

of little experiments on me. They took a sample from my leg. I have a scar on my thigh where they took a sample of tissue. They did something to my back and other things I'd rather not talk about."

In the past, these types of reports were dismissed as some sort of bizarre psychological aberration on the part of the "abductee." Only recently have researchers begun to consider the possibility that these claims are indeed true. Serious, painstaking studies by Pulitzer Prize winning Harvard psychiatrist Dr. John Mack, and Temple University professor of history Dr. David Jacobs, among others, have systematically docu-mented thousands of cases which have no ready explanation. Alien abduction believers claim that millions of Americans have been abducted aboard alien craft for physiological purposes. Ufologist Brian A. Borashas provided this humorous anecdote:

> Although no one can prove that people are actually taken aboard UFOs, if you should find yourself in this predicament, try to remain calm. Observe and remember as much as you can; even ask questions. Try to grab something and bring it back with you as evidence of your experience. As in life, having a sense of humor, and using your intelligence will help you deal with this most unusual situation.

On a more serious note, in October 1996 abductee expert Dr. David Jacobs was interviewed by the staff of the *Rutherford* magazine (a publication of the Rutherford Institute). Following are some excerpts from this most fascinating interview. Warning—what you are about to read may disturb you!

Rutherford: You've studied the abduction phenomenon for many years. How do you explain the abductees' accounts?

Jacobs: The abduction phenomenon is an alien-directed phenomenon. All the accounts I've looked at—about 650 over a ten-year period—have pointed in that direction. Some people think the government is in collusion with the aliens, but there is no evidence for this whatsoever.

Rutherford: What leads you to believe that this is an alien phenomenon?

Jacobs: You have to remember that all abduction cases are intertwined with the UFO phenomenon. Basically, the sighting of outside shells of objects has comprised the majority of the UFO mystery for years and years. But starting in 1961 with the case of Betty and Barney Hill, people began to come forward with accounts that suggested there was something going on inside the objects. Since then, tens of thousands of people have come forward and said that this thing has happened to them. And what is fascinating is that they all describe basically the same phenomenon, the same procedures, the same scenario. All of which points to a link to the UFO phenomenon—the goal of the UFOs is to abduct people for physiological purposes.

Rutherford: What kind of physiological purposes?

Jacobs: This is a reproductively oriented phenomenon, unfortunately. People routinely describe eggs being taken, sperm being taken, and women describe having fetuses implanted in them and having fetuses extracted. After a short time, they are allowed to view these babies, which look like a combination between human and alien. They call them "hybrids," and they are required to have some sort of skin-on-skin interaction with them for reasons we don't fully understand. We feel very strongly that the creation of these "hybrids" is what the abduction phenomenon is all about—a systematic program of physiological exploitation.

Rutherford: How many Americans do you think have experienced the abduction phenomenon?

Jacobs: I can't know that. The best we can do is ask indirect questions of the population to see how many have had abduction-like experiences even though they may not attribute them to the abduction phenomenon. We did that through a Roper poll in 1991. We came up with a minimum population of two percent of the American public, which seems like a small percentage but actually is about five million Americans. Now that's a very conservative number. We can't tell whether or not those people are abductees or not, because each case has to be investigated. The best we can say is that five million Americans, at least, have had experiences consistent with the experiences abductees have had.

Rutherford: How many cases have you personally investigated?

Jacobs: Hopkins (Budd Hopkins, the pioneer abduction researcher) and I have received over ten thousand letters and talked to maybe ten thousand more. Every single day we get letters and phone calls from abductees around the country.

Rutherford: Do you think this is a global phenomenon?

Jacobs: I can't say it's truly global because I don't know what's happening in Thailand, for example, or Burma. I do know that we have cases from Europe, Asia, Latin America, Africa, and Australia. Wherever you have large concentrations of people there seems to be the abduction-based phenomenon.

Rutherford: When did abduction claims start to surface?

Jacobs: We can only trace the abduction phenomenon back to around the turn of the century, perhaps 1896, 1897. Before that we lose sight of the abduction phenomenon. There is no serious evidence whatsoever before the late 1890s.

Rutherford: Do you think the abduction accounts point to something that we should fear?

Jacobs: I've gone round and round about this. I think the answer is yes. I think healthy fear is good in this particular area. It protects us a little bit, to be frightened, to be afraid. There are a lot of people who feel that this is a positive, wonderful phenomenon. I guarantee you that there is no serious evidence of this. When I see abductees, I look at people whose lives are shattered. I've seen people on the verge of suicide trying to get this phenomenon to stop. I've seen families torn apart. I've seen people just pleading—pleading with tears in their eyes—to help them stop this phenomenon.

Rutherford: So you don't agree with those who say this is a benevolent phenomenon?

Jacobs: I just don't see the evidence for this phenomenon to be cancer-curing, war-stopping, environment-helping. Humans would love to have this phenomenon be loving and caring and benevolent. This is a very, very human response and a cultural response to a large extent. I would like it to be wonderful, too. Unfortunately, I just don't find the spiritually uplifting phenomenon that some people just insist is there. These beings are not here to help us. They have their own agenda, and we are not allowed to know its full parameters. All we see of the visitors is a dispassionate clinical program fulfilling an agenda of their own that has very little to do with us except to use our bodies for their own purposes.

Rutherford: Do you think this is working toward an end?

Jacobs: Yes, it is. This is a program, and a program has a beginning, a middle, and an end. In my opinion we are in the end stage, or at least the end of the middle. I am very distressed by this phenomenon. When two societies meet each other, the ones with the inferior technology almost always suffer in one way or another. I have a feeling that might be the case with this phenomenon, and I think this is going to happen relatively soon.

Rutherford: So what do you think is going to happen?

Jacobs: I don't really know. I do feel that it relates ultimately to the little hybrid babies who grow up to be adults. We're going to be seeing a lot more hybrid adults directing abduction phenomena, and maybe even beginning to have more of a presence here in normal society.

Rutherford: Are you saying that within the next couple of decades human/alien hybrids will be mixing with our society?

Jacobs: That's what abductees indicate. I can't be sure of this. But the evidence certainly does point like an arrow to this kind of scenario. I know this is an extreme position, and a lot of people are going to disagree with me, but you have to go where the evidence leads you even though you may not like where it is going.

Rutherford: Has there been any physical evidence for this phenomenon other than the thousands of abduction accounts?

Jacobs: There is quite a lot of physical evidence. People have come back with odd scars and marks on their bodies which were not there the day before. They have come back with unusual implants in nasal passages, in their ears, in other parts of their bodies. People come back with unusual stains on their clothes from certain physical procedures that are done to them. There are marks on people's grounds. They say a UFO landed outside, and there is a huge mark on their lawn—burned and broken grass, or dehydrated ground, or baked soil. Not only that, when people say they are abducted, they are physically missing from their normal environments. Police are called, search parties have been sent out, children have been missing, parents have been frantic. Even more, there are multiple abductions. People see each other being abducted.

Rutherford: What, in your opinion, is the strongest evidence for the abduction phenomenon?

Jacobs: It is the precision of detail. The convergence of stories by people who come from all walks of life, all levels of education, across ethnic groups, across racial groups, across religious groups, across culture, educational, economic groups, all of whom say the same thing. These are not vague stories. These stories are extremely precise and go from A to B to C to D all the way from beginning to end, all saying essentially the same thing in great detail.

Rutherford: But aren't there psychological explanations for the abduction accounts?

Jacobs: Unfortunately, no. When members of the scientific community take a look at this, the first thing they think of is the wide, wide range of psychological, cultural, and psychiatric explanations. What they don't understand is that we have spent the last thirty years looking at every conceivable kind of cultural, psychological, and psychiatric explanation. All the way from the current trendy repressed memories to just plain lying for some reason or another and everything in between. Nobody in their right minds would just jump in the 1960s or the 1970s and say that this is actually happening to people. No psychological, psychiatric, or cultural explanation fits the data. If it did, we would leap for it. No significant body of thought has come about that presents strong evidence of anything happening other than what the abductees have stated.

I tend to agree with ufologist Tom Cousineau's assessment of Dr. Jacob's research. According to Cousineau:

Jacob's study edges past the standard academic commentary and into an old prophet's warning of an alien invasion that is already under way, one we don't take seriously at our own peril.

Harvard psychiatrist Dr. John Mack has come to the exact same disturbing conclusion:

The only theory that makes any sense is that what's happening is exactly what the people say is happening to them. Namely, that some kind of entity, some kind of intelligence, is coming into our world, taking people, and doing things.

In the sequel to his bestselling book *Chariots of the Gods?* entitled *Return of the Gods,* Swiss ufologist Erich von Daniken has this to say about the UFO abduction phenomenon:

So what's going on? The researches of Dr. Fieberg in German-speaking countries are paralleled by investigations by David Jacobs of America. He believes that the sperm extractions and artificial fertilizations are the reason for all the abductions, the aim being to create a half-human, half-alien life-form. The reported cases are increasing; there are not hundreds but thousands of them. So is it just a passing craze? If so, why suddenly now? Have thousands of people who do not even know each other, who live on different

continents, suddenly all been infected by the same madness?
Do all these cases have a psychological explanation?

"No, they do not," says someone whose views we should respect. Dr. John Mack is a top psychologist and professor of
psychiatry at the most renowned university in America—
Harvard. Professor Mack is not only a psychologist and psychiatrist, but also an experienced doctor at the Cambridge
Hospital in Massachusetts, and winner of the highly sought-
after Pulitzer Prize. Dr. Mack, who is in his mid-sixties, knows
his profession and is quick to see through the tricks, lies, and
fantasies of his subjects. In 1989 Dr. Mack was asked whether
he was interested in treating some people who said that they
had been abducted by aliens. Mack's reaction was that "they
must be mad." At a later date Dr. Mack made the acquain-
tance of American abduction expert Budd Hopkins, author
of the bestselling book on alien abductions entitled *Intruders.*
This encounter would change Dr. Mack's life. In the next few
years Professor Mack met with hundreds of people from various regions of the country who had never had any contact
with each other. All of these individuals had claimed an abduction experience. According to Dr. Mack these people appeared to him to be absolutely sane, reasonable, and reliable.
Slowly, Dr. Mack's interest in the abduction phenomenon
began to intensify. At last, Dr. Mack undertook a thorough
study involving seventy-eight abduction victims, subjecting
them to all of the rigorous tests and procedures of his profession. The results of this research are now available in a 400-
page book written by Dr. Mack entitled *Abduction: Human
Encounters with Aliens.* According to Dr. Mack:

> Yes, the extraterrestrials exist; the abductees are telling the
> truth, and embryo extractions, sperm-sample taking, and
> artificial fertilization have all taken place. These are not psy-
> chological delusions or wish-fulfillment fantasies. We are

clearly participants in a universe that is swarming with intelligent life-forms, from whom we have cut ourselves off.

In his book, Professor Mack explains that abductions always follow the same general pattern:

Small beings with large, black, vertically positioned eyes and grayish skin are suddenly seen moving about in a bedroom as if they have come through the walls (abductions from cars have also been known to occur). The aliens have small nostrils and tiny mouths with narrow lips. There are often curious lights to be seen outside. The abduction victims feel fear and panic and start imagining all sorts of horrific things. But they are calmed, made cold, and physically paralyzed. Then begins a spectral flight through the window or the balcony door; and although some victims feel that they are being beamed up, they sense the currents of the night air around them. They arrive at a spacecraft. Inside it is bright; they are laid upon some kind of operating table and investigated with unrecognizable instruments. Hair and skin samples are removed, fine needles and other objects are inserted into their bodily orifices. Around the table stand several of the little gray people, but it always seems that only one fulfills the function of "chief surgeon," while another takes the role of "translator." Very seldom is there any spoken exchange—communication takes place by means of telepathy.

This treatment by the abducting aliens can be very unpleasant and is often described as "repulsive." Physical pain, however, is rarely felt, for the aliens neutralize the pain center of the brain. After this "operation," a dialogue often takes place, during which the abductors try, at least in a fragmentary way, to explain their action to their victims. Some abductees are shown whole shelves of small embryos, which float in some kind of fluid. The abductee reaches home again in the same way that they left.

Of course we easily dismiss these stories—they sound ridiculous, far-fetched, and strange. However, Dr. Mack, a Harvard-trained physician and Nobel Prize recipient, is a firm believer in the reality of these abduction cases. Thomas Bullard, writing for the *International UFO Reporter,* has said:

> Abductions may or may not represent literal contacts with aliens, but whatever they are, they constitute a strange phenomenon worthy of study from a number of perspectives and by diverse disciplines. . . . Whatever their physical nature, even if they prove to be nothing more than stars and airplanes, their cultural impact has been enormous.

According to UFO researcher John Weldon, the abduction phenomenon is in reality an occultic phenomenon:

> People who claim to experience alien abductions are in essence dabbling in the occult. They may be doing this innocently or not, but because of its impact on a person's life—an impact which can continue for years—an alien abduction experience certainly may end up going into contactee stature and even possession. . . . I believe an alleged alien abduction is basically an experience that is implanted into the mind. It's like what a hypnotist can do with a certain percentage of the population. They can make an individual think or do things that they ordinarily would not do.

Long-time UFO researcher John Keel notes a high number of fatalities among those dabbling in UFO contacts. Author William Alnor, in his excellent book entitled *UFOs in the New Age,* says this:

> I believe that something very strange indeed is happening throughout the world today. In the late 1940s began what we refer to as the modern UFO era, when people worldwide reported having seen shiny disks whiz across the sky.

The 1950s saw people claiming to be contactees for alien civilizations from within our solar system (mostly Venus). In the 1970s and 1980s increasing numbers of people claimed to have been abducted by aliens from other star systems. And late in the 1980s an increasing number of UFO enthusiasts began joining the New Age movement.

Investigative journalist Stuart Goldman has this to say about the abduction phenomenon:

> In looking at the backgrounds of the UFO abductees, it quickly becomes clear that almost to a man, they have some background in New Age or occultic beliefs. Interestingly, studies show that there are very few practicing Christians or Jews among UFO contactees. What could this mean? Are the aliens racist? Or does this, rather, indicate something about the belief systems of the abductees themselves?

In his best-selling book *Abduction,* Dr. John Mack quotes one of his clients as saying ominously, in a tone that recalls our ancestors talking about the gods or our fate:

> Something else is interested in us that we don't want to know about. . . . This is really a responsibility, and things that you don't want to see happen are going to happen.

Wow! What are we to make of all of this ? We have seen the scientific evidence proving the existence of UFOs. We have heard the eyewitness accounts. We have seen that supernatural/demonic forces are at work behind the UFO phenomenon. We have examined the abduction phenomenon. We have heard from the secular experts. Let's now focus our attention on the Bible and see what the Word of God has to say about the UFO enigma.

Chapter Seven

UFOs and the Bible?

And it came to pass, when the LORD would take up Elijah into heaven by a whirlwind, that Elijah went with Elisha from Gilgal. . . . And it came to pass, as they still went on, and talked, that, behold, there appeared a chariot of fire, and horses of fire, and parted them both asunder; and Elijah went up by a whirlwind into heaven. And Elisha saw it, and he cried, My father, my father, the chariot of Israel, and the horsemen thereof. And he saw him no more: and he took hold of his own clothes, and rent them in two pieces.

—2 Kings 2:1,11–12

In building their argument proving the existence of UFOs, secular experts often point to the Bible for support. In the UFO Enigma Museum in Roswell, New Mexico, there is an exhibit citing the biblical passages that ufologists believe refer to UFOs. They highlight six main scriptural passages to bolster their view:

1. Genesis 6:1–4 (the sons of God)
2. Exodus 14:19–20,24–25 (the pillar of cloud and fire in the wilderness)
3. Second Kings 2:9–10 (the "abduction" of Elijah into the heavens)
4. Ezekiel 1:4–7 (the vision of a flying throne chariot)
5. Zechariah 5:1–2 (the flying scroll—a cylindrical UFO)
6. Matthew 2:9–10 (the Bethlehem star)

Let's look briefly at each of these passages to see if they are describing a UFO incident.

Pillars of Cloud and Fire

During the exodus and the time of wandering in the wilderness, God protected and guided the children of Israel by direct supernatural means.

> And the LORD went before them by day in a pillar of a cloud, to lead them the way; and by night in a pillar of fire, to give them light; to go by day and night: He took not away the pillar of the cloud by day, nor the pillar of fire by night, from before the people. . . . And the angel of God, which went before the camp of Israel, removed and went behind them; and the pillar of the cloud went from before their face, and stood behind them: And it came between the camp

of the Egyptians and the camp of Israel; and it was a cloud and darkness to them, but it gave light by night to these: so that the one came not near the other all the night. . . . And it came to pass, that in the morning watch the LORD looked unto the host of the Egyptians through the pillar of fire and of the cloud, and troubled the host of the Egyptians,

—Exodus 13:21–22; 14:19–20,24

And it came to pass on the twentieth day of the second month, in the second year, that the cloud was taken up from off the tabernacle of the testimony. And the children of Israel took their journeys out of the wilderness of Sinai; and the cloud rested in the wilderness of Paran.

—Numbers 10:11–12

These passages of Scripture clearly reveal to any objective reader that the pillar of the cloud and fire were divine intervention in the lives of His people and not UFOs.

Chariots of Fire

Elijah was one of the great prophets of Israel in the ninth century B.C. during the wicked reign of King Ahab. After appointing his successor to the prophetic office, Elijah was led out into the wilderness near Jericho and was translated to heaven in a chariot of fire. Ufologists contend that Elijah was one of the earliest recorded UFO abductees. However, the biblical account makes it quite clear that Elijah was translated to heaven by the Lord.

And it came to pass, when the LORD would take up Elijah into heaven by a whirlwind, that Elijah went with Elisha from Gilgal. . . . And it came to pass, as they still went on, and talked, that, behold, there appeared a chariot of fire, and horses of fire, and parted them both asunder; and Elijah went up by a whirlwind into heaven. And Elisha saw it,

and he cried, My father, my father, the chariot of Israel,
and the horsemen thereof. And he saw him no more: and
he took hold of his own clothes, and rent them in two pieces.

—2 Kings 2:1,11–12

We also know that Elijah was not abducted by a UFO because
he later appeared with the Lord Himself on the Mount of
Transfiguration in Matthew 17, and according to Malachi 4,
he will come again to Earth before the great and terrible day
of the Lord. Elijah, like Enoch, was translated directly to
heaven without tasting physical death. As such, he is a beautiful picture of the coming Rapture of the Church when millions of living saints will be instantaneously translated to
heaven in glorified bodies (1 Cor. 15:50–54; 1 Thess. 4:13–
18)

The Throne Chariot

Ezekiel 1 is an amazing chapter. Ezekiel, who was carried
away to Babylon in 597 B.C. in the second deportation, is by
the river Chebar in the middle of the summer of 593 B.C. As
he looks off toward the north he sees an object coming toward him that was unlike anything he had ever seen. I would
like to cite the entire chapter at this point because its description is so strange and specific, however, I will only cite a few
specific passages.

> And I looked, and, behold, a whirlwind came out of the
> north, a great cloud, and a fire infolding itself, and a bright-
> ness was about it, and out of the midst thereof as the color
> of amber, out of the midst of the fire. Also out of the midst
> thereof came the likeness of four living creatures. And this
> was their appearance; they had the likeness of a man. And
> every one had four faces, and every one had four wings. . . .
> As for the likeness of their faces, they four had the face of a
> man, and the face of a lion, on the right side: and they four

had the face of an ox on the left side; they four also had the face of an eagle. . . . As for the likeness of the living creatures, their appearance was like burning coals of fire, and like the appearance of lamps: it went up and down among the living creatures; and the fire was bright, and out of the fire went forth lightning. . . . And when the living creatures went, the wheels went by them: and when the living creatures were lifted up from the earth, the wheels were lifted up. . . . And the likeness of the firmament upon the heads of the living creature was as the colour of the terrible crystal, stretched forth over their heads above. . . . And when they went, I heard the noise of their wings, like the noise of great waters, as the voice of the Almighty, the voice of speech, as the noise of an host: when they stood, they let down their wings. . . . And above the firmament that was over their heads was the likeness of a throne, as the appearance of a sapphire stone: and upon the likeness of the throne was the likeness as the appearance of a man above upon it. And I saw as the colour of amber, as the appearance of fire round about within it, from the appearance of his loins even upward, and from the appearance of his loins even downward, I saw as it were the appearance of fire, and it had brightness round about. As the appearance of the bow that is in the cloud in the day of rain, so was the appearance of the brightness round about. This was the appearance of the likeness of the glory of the LORD. And when I saw it, I fell upon my face, and I heard a voice of one that spake.

—Ezekiel 1:4–6,10,13,19,22,24,26–28

This bizarre scene certainly sounds like many modern UFO sightings—a kaleidoscope of whirling wheels, bright lights, dazzling colors, and strange beings with four-sided faces. It sounds like something straight out of the "X-Files." However, this passage records Ezekiel's commission to God's service as a prophet and a theophany (an appearance of God in visionary form). This is the ultimate UFO—a visible manifestation of God Himself riding His throne chariot across the desert sky of Babylon in the middle of the summer. As Nahum 1:3, reminds us, "the clouds are the dust of his feet."

The strange living creatures described in the early part of the chapter are a special order of angelic beings called cherubim that are the special bearers of God's throne chariot. As they move about transporting the throne chariot of God, there is a cacophany of sound like water rushing down a mountain stream and as intense as the voice of God.

Ezekiel did indeed see and hear something from "another world." He saw the "appearance of the likeness of the glory of the Lord." Note his response at the end of Ezekiel 1:28: "And when I saw it, I fell upon my face, and I heard a voice of one that spake." Ezekiel fell prostrate before the Lord of Glory. So should we!

The Flying Scroll

The prophet Zechariah is one of the most enigmatic Old Testament writers. In the first six chapters he relates eight visions; in chapters seven and eight, four messages; and in nine through fourteen, two burdens. One of the visions is that of a flying scroll in 5:1–3.

> Then I turned, and lifted up mine eyes, and looked, and behold a flying roll. And he said unto me, What seest thou? And I answered, I see a flying roll; the length thereof is twenty cubits, and the breadth thereof ten cubits. Then said he unto me, This is the curse that goeth forth over the face of the whole earth: for every one that stealeth shall be cut off as on this side according to it; and every one that sweareth shall be cut off as on that side according to it.

In interpreting Zechariah's visions one must remember that he is employing highly symbolic language. The last three visions have to do with the administration of God's judgment. The vision of the flying scroll is both simple and severe. The fact that the scroll has writing on both sides is reminiscent of language describing the two tablets of the law (Exod. 32:15). The curse of the scroll is directed toward violators of the middle command of each of the two tablets—the eighth commandment against stealing, and the third commandment against swearing falsely by misusing the name of the Lord. The objects of the curse in verse three represent all those who violate the law of God.

The flying scroll then is not a UFO, but a symbol of God's judgment against all who violate His law.

Let the reader beware!

The Bethlehem . . . UFO?

Matthew 2 records the birth of the Lord Jesus Christ into this world and the response of the world to His coming. While Herod is *antagonistic* and the religious leaders are *apathetic*, the magi come from over one thousand miles away in Parthia (modern northeast Iran) over difficult terrain to *adore* Him.

But why did they come? What led them to Jerusalem? A star. What star?

There are over five hundred books on the subject of the Bethlehem "star." There are numerous natural explanations.

1. Halley's comet (12 B.C.)
2. Kepler discovered a conjunction of Jupiter and Saturn in October–November 7 B.C. Jupiter is the king of the planets and Saturn is the star of the Jews. The conjunction occurred in the constellation Pisces (the fish) the symbol of early Christianity.
3. Kepler preferred the view that it was a supernova.
4. There are a number of other planetary conjuctions that have been suggested.
5. A UFO

There are also two supernatural explanations.

1. A supernatural star
2. The Shekinah glory of God

The best interpetation is that the "star" is the glory of God, the same glory that shone around the shepherds in Luke 2:9. The Greek word *aster* from which we get our word "asteroid" is used figuratively to represent any great brilliance or radiance. There are numerous examples in the Scriptures of God's light appearing to men: the Shekinah glory in the Old Testament; Saul on the road to Damascus (Acts 9); Jesus' transfiguration (Matt. 17); John on Patmos (Rev. 1:16); the sign of the Son of Man (Matt. 24:30).

Several other factors point to this interpretation as the best solution. First, the wise men said they saw the star "in the east" (Matt. 2:2) and that they did not see it again until they were on their way to Bethlehem (v. 9). Second, the star came and stood over the house where Jesus was marking it as the place of his abode (v. 9). Both of these facts seem inconsistent with any natural explanation or any special "star."

The Bethlehem "star" was certainly not a UFO in the modern sense of the term. It was the glory of God appearing to these magi in the east and directing them to Jerusalem. When they discovered from the Jewish leaders that the Messiah would be born in Bethlehem, they set out and the light appeared to them again and guided them to the exact house where Jesus was living.

Sons of God

One of the key Old Testament passages that always surfaces in any serious discussion of UFOs and the Bible is Genesis 6:1–4. This is one of the most mysterious sections of the Bible. It describes the marriage of "the sons of God" to the "daughters of men," and calls their progeny the "nephilim," or giants. Who were these sons of God? Why were their children singled out as "mighty men of old, men of renown"? Why did God send the flood to wipe them out? Were the sons of God men, or beings from another world?

The next chapter will answer these questions. You will be amazed at what we discover about these sons of God.

Chapter Eight

One GIANT Leap
for
Mankind

Before the flood, thou with thy lusty crew,
False titled sons of God, roaming the earth,
Cast wanton eyes on the daughters of men,
And coupled with them, and begot a race.

— John Milton, *Paradise Regained*

Ancient Mystery

Of all the biblical passages that could possibly refer to extraterrestrial encounters and/or UFOs, Genesis 6:1–5 is by far the most intriguing and, at the same time, the most troubling. In this passage we find recorded the account of the unimaginable union between fallen angelic beings and human women. Let's look at this most amazing passage more closely to see if any clues to the cosmic riddle of the UFO might be hidden in this ancient Hebrew text.

> And it came to pass, when men began to multiply on the face of the earth, and daughters were born unto them, That the sons of God saw the daughters of men that they were fair; and they took them wives of all which they chose. . . . There were giants in the earth in those days; and also after that, when the sons of God came in unto the daughters of men, and they bare children to them, the same became mighty men which were of old, men of renown. And God saw that the wickedness of man was great in the earth, and that every imagination of the thoughts of his heart was only evil continually.
>
> —Genesis 6:1–5

The exact meaning of this passage has been hotly debated by Bible scholars over the centuries. There are basically four schools of interpretation:

The Non-Literal View

At first glance, this passage reminds one of the legends, superstitions, and myths of old—the tales of the gods coming down and cohabitating with human women and producing some kind of hybrid, superhuman offspring. Therefore, many readers simply dismiss this passage altogether as just another example of the strange non-literal mythology of antiquity.

The Sethite View

Others look at this passage and attempt to desupernaturalize it in order to make it more intellectually palatable. Bible students in this camp explain the "sons of God" as rebellious descendants of the godly line of Seth, and the "daughters of men" as ungodly descendants of Cain. Therefore, the union between these two lines marks the end of separation between believers and unbelievers. This indiscriminate intermarrying between the godly line of Seth and the ungodly descendants of Cain caused the degeneration of the pure godly line in the antediluvian world. The offspring of these unholy unions became tyrants. Bible commentator Matthew Henry best represents this view:

> The sons of Seth (that is the professors of religion) married the daughters of men, that is, those that were profane, and strangers to God and godliness. The posterity of Seth did not keep by themselves, as they ought to have done, they intermingled themselves with the excommunicated race of Cain.

The Ambitious Despot View

Under this view, ancient power-hungry despots who were most likely of the Cainite line began to practice gross polygamy in order to expand their individual dominion. Scholars in this camp assume that the Hebrew word *elohim* could be translated as either "God" or "ruler." Others who hold to this view assume that the ancient Near Eastern cultures viewed "rulers" as "sons of God." Thus the phrase "sons of God" is essentially an ancient Near Eastern title for nobles, aristocrats, and kings. These ambitious despots lusted after power and wealth and desired to become "men of renown." Their sin was not intermarriage between two religious communities (Sethite and Cainite), but rather the sin of polygamy. This view arose within rabbinical circles during the middle of the second century A.D., partly, it seems, out of conviction that angels could not indulge in sexual intercourse, and partly to suppress speculation about them.

The problem with these first three interpretations of Genesis 6:1–5 is that they do not adequately explain why the progeny of such unions would be referred to as "giants," or why their presence would lead to a universal increase in sin and wickedness upon the Earth, and ultimately God's cataclysmic judgment via the flood. The fourth and final view best accounts for all these factors.

The Fallen Angel View

The obvious and natural reading of Genesis 6:1–5 seems to indicate that during the days of Noah, a bizarre and abominable atrocity transpired, something so horrible, something so unthinkable, that it in turn led to a tidal wave of wickedness overflowing the Earth. This corruption of planet Earth during Noah's day was so extensive that no normal remedy would suffice. Only utter destruction could properly eradicate this terrible infestation of wickedness. This unprecedented sin was that the "sons of God" (fallen angelic beings) saw the "daughters of men" and took them as their wives. The offspring from this ungodly union were "giants," men of renown, monsters not only in size, but in wickedness as well. Like an invading armada of extraterrestrial aliens, these fallen angels lusted after earthly women and, therefore, left their proper abode in the heavenlies and came storming to Earth in order to consummate their desire for strange flesh. Bible commentator W. R. Newell states the case clearly:

> There is no possible explanation of these verses except the fact of an invasion of human beings, by beings of another order (. . . who were, alas, fallen angels that kept not their own principality but left their proper habitation).

Back to the Future

Interestingly, the characteristics of those antediluvian days, strange as they may seem to our enlightened minds today, are nevertheless prophesied to be repeated during the final days of this present age. In Matthew 24:3, just two days before Christ's death on the cross, Jesus' disciples asked Him: "What shall be the sign of thy coming, and of the end of the world?" Jesus' response to this question pointed to a number of "signs" (wars, rumors of wars, earthquakes, famines, etc.), all of which would occur in that "generation" that would witness His return. However, these general signs were climaxed with a strange prophetic warning found in Matthew 24:37–39:

> But as the days of Noe were, so shall also the coming of the Son of man be. For as in the days that were before the flood they were eating and drinking, marrying and giving in marriage, until the day that Noe entered into the ark, And knew not until the flood came, and took them all away; so shall also the coming of the Son of man be.

In these verses Jesus not only verifies the historicity of the great flood, but He also instructs us to study closely the characteristics of the days just before the flood, because those days would be eerily similar to the days just before His return. So what was it about the days of Noah that made them so unique? What type of activity was going on in Noah's day that we see reoccurring in our day? Two answers come to mind:

1. The unprecedented sin and moral wickedness of man (Gen. 6:5).
2. The unprecedented overt invasion of fallen angelic beings to planet Earth (Gen. 6:1–4).

So it was the wickedness of humanity combined with the abominable union of the supernatural with the natural that moved God to judge the world. Are we fast approaching a repeat performance of the days of Noah? Are the "sons of God" once again invading planet Earth? Could the burgeoning of UFO activity in our time be proof of our proximity to the "last days"? The key to answering these questions lies in the proper interpretation of Genesis 6. Are the "sons of God" really fallen angelic beings, or are they simply the "godly sons of Seth"? If we can show that the "sons of God" are indeed fallen angelic beings, then we will have established a crucial link between Genesis 6 and the demonic hypothesis explaining the origin and nature of UFOs and their occupants. This would be one **giant** leap for mankind. Let's take a look at the evidence for interpreting Genesis 6:1–5 as a reference to an antediluvian alien/demonic invasion of planet Earth.

The Clear Meaning of "bene elohim"

The first and most important piece of evidence that we need to examine is the meaning of the Hebrew phrase "sons of God." The actual phrase in the Hebrew is *bene elohim,* and it is used only four other times in the Old Testament. Three of these occurrences are in the book of Job (1:6; 2:1; 38:7). Job 1:6 is representative of these verses and reads as follows:

> Now there was a day when the sons of God came to present themselves before the LORD, and Satan came also among them.

There can be no doubt at all that in each of these passages in Job, the meaning of *bene elohim* applies exclusively to angels. The fourth Old Testament occurrence of the phrase "son(s) of God" is found in the book of Daniel where we are told of Nebuchadnezzar that he saw four men walking in his burning, fiery furnace. He recognized three of them as his human victims (Shadrach, Meshach, and Abednego). However the fourth was "like a son of God" (in this case, it was a preincarnate appearance of the Lord Jesus Christ).

It is quite clear then, that the use of the title "sons of God" in the Old Testament is confined to angelic beings and to Christ. Thus, there seems to be no reasonable doubt that, in so far as the Hebrew language is concerned, the intent of the writer of Genesis 6 was most likely to convey the thought of angels. Bible commentator Arno C. Gaebelein has stated:

> The question is, who are the sons of God who took the daughters of men. . . . "Sons of God" is the term applied in the Old Testament to supernatural beings, both good and evil. Angels good and fallen are termed sons of God in the Old Testament. Satan himself is reckoned among the sons of God in Job 1:6 and 2:1. The term "sons of God" must mean here supernatural evil beings. These evil beings came down out of the air and began to take possession of such of the daughters of men as they chose.

In his book entitled *Spiritism and the Fallen Angels,* James M. Gray says this about the term "sons of God":

> We find that "sons of God" is used everywhere in the Old Testament to designate angels, and why should it not be used here? Moreover, if it were so used, it would carry with it a confounding of two distinct orders of creatures and the production of a mixed race, partly human, partly superhuman, which would be just such a derangement of the Divine plan as to warrant that which occurred, namely, the almost total extermination of all who were upon the Earth.

It is also interesting to note that neither the descendants of Seth, or any other true believers for that matter, are ever referred to in the book of Genesis as "sons of God." In fact, "believers" are never called "sons of God" in the Old Testament. For human beings, "sonship" is a concept that is unique to the New Testament.

From this evidence, one must conclude that the only natural and obvious understanding of this phrase, "sons of God," is that these beings were angelic sons of God rather than men. God refers to them as His "sons" because they had been directly created by God and were not born of their own order.

The Clear Translation of the Greek Septuagint

The Greek Septuagint is a translation of the Old Testament from Hebrew to Greek around the year 280 B.C. It is very significant that the Septuagint renders the Genesis 6:2 phrase *bene elohim* as "angels of God." This fact is significant simply due to the age of the Septuagint. Secondly, this fact is important because the Septuagint was the most commonly used version of the Old Testament during the apostolic period. The Septuagint would have been the Greek-language Old Testament read and quoted by Christ and His apostles during the first century A.D. In other words, the Septuagint has been proven to be a reliable translation of the Old Testament for some twenty-three hundred years.

Ancient Consensus

The "angel" interpretation of Genesis 6 is both the oldest view and the view held by most modern commentators. The colorful first century Jewish historian Flavius Josephus, as well as almost all other ancient Jewish writers and interpreters, as well as the earliest Christian writers, all held that the Genesis 6:2 phrase, *bene elohim,* was a reference to fallen angels. Men like Philo, Justin Martyr, Clement of Alexandria, Origen, Iraneaus, Cyprian, Tertullian, Ambrose, Methodius, etc., all agree that the Hebrew phrase "sons of God" is a reference to fallen angels. In his monumental work *Antiquities of the Jews,* Josephus elaborates on the ancient tradition of fallen angels cohabitating with human women prior to the flood:

Many angels of God accompanied with women, and begat

sons that proved unjust, and despisers of all that was good, on account of their strength. . . . These men did what resembled the acts of those whom the Grecians called giants. . . . There was till then left the race of giants, who had bodies so large, and countenances so entirely different from other men, that they were surprising to the sight, and terrible to the hearing. The bones of these men are still shown to this very day.

Justin Martyr, who lived between A.D. 110 and 165, provides us with the same commentary on the antediluvian culture: "The angels transgressed, and were captivated by love for women and begat children."

The ancient apocryphal books of First Enoch, Jubilees, and the Apocalypse of Baruch, as well as certain writings within the Dead Sea Scrolls, equate the activity of Genesis 6 with fallen angels and discuss at great length the descent of the angelic "Watchers" and their giant progeny. In one such reference in the book of First Enoch, God instructs Enoch as follows:

Go, say to the Watchers of heaven, who have sent thee to intercede for them: "Ye should intercede for men, and not men for you. Wherefore have ye left high, holy and eternal heaven, and lain with women and defiled yourselves with the daughters of men, and taken wives unto yourselves and done like the children of earth and begotten giants as sons. And although ye were holy, spiritual living and eternal life, you have defiled yourselves with the blood of women, and have begotten children with the blood of flesh, have lusted after flesh and blood as those who do die and perish."

It seems the church fathers in the first four centuries knew no other interpretation except that the "sons of God" were angels. In fact, the first Christian writers to suggest the Sethite interpretation were Chrysostom and Augustine (fourth century A.D.). This interpretation ruled the day, and for the past fifteen hundred years many Bible scholars have held that the "sons of God" referred to in Genesis 6 are the godly sons of Seth and that "the daughters of men" are the wicked daughters of Cain. They have adopted this interpretation in part because the "fallen angel" alternative seems so bizarre and outlandish to them. However, the ancient interpretation (in our opinion, the correct one) is that the "sons of God" were fallen angels who came down to Earth and lusted after the daughters of men and married them, thus producing this amazing hybrid progeny that the Bible calls "giants."

Marriages Not Made in Heaven

Although Scripture teaches that believers should not marry unbelievers (1 Cor. 7:39; 2 Cor. 6:14), there is no hint that this particular sin would be unforgivable or more responsible for producing societal deterioration than other sin. Also, there is no medical evidence whatsoever that a believer marrying an unbeliever causes "giantism" in the children produced from such a union. Also, the flood would have been a bit too harsh of a punishment for this type of sin. If the events of Genesis 6 are to be interpreted as just a case of mixed marriages between good men and wicked women, it would be surprising indeed that God would have issued the severe judgment that He did. It would seem that something far more sinister is being referred to in this passage.

The Question of Angels and Sex

Another reason some refuse to accept the fallen angel interpretation of Genesis 6 is because they feel it would be impossible for angels to have sexual relations with human women and to father children by them. However, this objection presupposes more about the abilities of angels than we really know. It is true that Jesus said in Matthew 22:30 that "in the resurrection they neither marry, nor are given in marriage, but are as the angels of God in heaven." However, this is far from saying that angels themselves are "sexless." Surely human beings who share in the resurrection will retain their own personal identity, including their male or female gender. Furthermore, when Jesus said that the angels of God in heaven do not marry, this did not mean that those angels who had been cast out of heaven were incapable of doing so. In his book entitled *Satan,* author F. C. Jennings has this to say about angels and sex:

> There may be physiological difficulties; but we know so little of the possibilities of angelic existence that we may well leave this. That angels should eat and drink; feed on meat and bread; might certainly involve equal difficulties, but it is clearly stated in Genesis 18 and 19. Thus angels appear to have a power of materializing, and assuming the functions of a human body.

The New Testament book of Jude seems to be quite explicit that these fallen angels did indeed take on or possibly even take over human bodies and give themselves over to strange flesh. Jude 6–7 states:

> And the angels which kept not their first estate, but left their own habitation, he hath reserved in everlasting chains under darkness unto the judgment of the great day. Even as Sodom and Gomorrha, and the cities about them in like manner, giving themselves over to fornication, and going after strange flesh, are set forth for an example, suffering the vengeance of eternal fire.

It is interesting that whenever angels have appeared visibly to men, as recorded in the Bible, they always appear in the physical bodies of men. Do you remember the angels who appeared to Abraham in Genesis 18—they appeared in the form of men. Later in that same story, these angels went to Sodom to retrieve Lot and his family, and the men of Sodom were attempting to seize these two "men" and use them for their homosexual purposes. Jude says that in just the same way that the men of Sodom went after strange flesh, so these fallen angels pursued strange flesh as well.

It seems apparent from Scripture that God has given angels the capacity of materializing themselves into masculine human form whenever the occasion warrants. While it was clearly not God's intention or will that angels mix in a sexual way with human women, the bottom line is that fallen angels have no regard or concern for the expressed will of God. In fact, it was probably precisely for the purpose of thwarting God's will that this particular rogue battalion of the "sons of God" engaged in these forbidden sexual relationships with human women. One commentator writes:

> Satan had not forgotten God's prophecy that a promised Seed of the woman would one day destroy him. . . . . Satan and his angels must have feared that their opportunities for victory in the cosmic conflict were in imminent danger. Desiring reinforcements for a coming battle against the hosts of heaven, and also desiring, if possible to completely corrupt mankind before the promised "Seed" could accomplish Satan's defeat, they seem to have decided to utilize the marvelous power of procreation which God had given the human family and corrupt it to their own ends. Men were now rapidly multiplying on the Earth and by implanting their own "seed" in humanity, they might be able to enlist in only one generation a vast multitude as allies against God.

The "Not So Godly" Line of Seth

If the Hebrew phrase *bene elohim* is indeed a reference to the godly line of Seth, then that presupposes that the line of Seth was godly. The obvious problem is that the sons of Seth were certainly not all godly men (remember—all of them with the exception of Noah and his family perished in the flood), so why should they be called the "sons of God"? It is also important to remember that Adam and Eve had many more sons in addition to Cain and Seth. Were these spiritual "sons of God" like Seth, or were they ungodly like Cain?

Furthermore, feminists would ask, "Why all this focus on the union of godly men with ungodly women? What about the godly women marrying ungodly men?"

Finally, if Moses (the author of Genesis 6) wanted us to know that the sons of Seth began to marry the daughters of Cain, why did he not just simply say so and thus avoid all of the confusion?

The Folklore and Fable Connection

Another bit of interesting evidence pointing to the "fallen angel" interpretation in Genesis 6, is the abundance of folklore, myths, legends, fables, etc., that speak of "gods" coming down to the Earth in ancient times and having sexual relations with human women. Marriages between the daughters of men and the gods are a well-known feature of Greek, Egyptian, Ugaritic, Canaanite, Hurrian, and Mesopotamian theology and/or mythology. Even the heroic figure of Gilgamesh (the hero of the Babylonian flood epic) was the product of such a union.

Ancient mythology is literally full of incidents which reflect a direct parallel between the scriptural account found in Genesis 6. Hercules, the mighty strongman of antiquity, for example, was alleged to have been born of the illicit union of Zeus and a beautiful young maiden named Alcmene. Aztec traditions tell of a race of wicked antediluvian giants of supernatural origin; the Persian sacred books refer to the corruption of the world by "Ahriman" and the punishment of the people's iniquity by a great rainstorm. Similar traditions are found in North America, India, and China.

It's been well said that mythology and folklore are "thought- fossils" depicting the story of vanished cultures in symbols and allegories. We are all acquainted with the extensive mythologies and legends from ancient Greece, Rome, etc. In these mythologies the gods come down to Earth to partake in sex orgies, promiscuities, cruelties, and violence of all kinds. Most historians agree that mythology is based on ancient traditions that have at least some historical base—some kernel of historical truth. The hideous creatures and gods worshipped by the ancient Greeks, Romans, Sumerians, etc., could have had their beginnings in the "sons of God," "giants," and "men of renown," mentioned in Genesis 6. Christian author and spokesman Francis Schaeffer has said:

> More and more we are finding that mythology in general, though greatly contorted, very often has some historic base. And the interesting thing is that one myth that occurs over and over again in many parts of the world is that somewhere, a long time ago, supernatural beings had sexual intercourse with natural women and produced a special breed of people.

Future Shock

It seems clear from this evidence that the "sons of God" mentioned in Genesis 6 were indeed fallen angels. These particular satanic angels further compounded their original sin of following Satan in his rebellion against God by abandoning "their own habitation" and "keeping not their first estate" and "going after strange flesh." The specific sin of these invading extraterrestrials was so repugnant and so vile that the Bible says that God no longer allows this specific group of fallen angels to roam the Earth like other demons, but rather He has confined them according to 2 Peter 2:4 "into chains of darkness, to be reserved unto judgment."

So it seems that beings from space did indeed arrive on planet Earth during the days of Noah. These were fallen spiritual beings whose sin of cohabitating with human women was so wicked and so utterly repulsive that it moved God to unleash the most devastating judgment the world had ever experienced—the flood. It may very well be that this particular feature of the days of Noah is beginning to be repeated in the current global proliferation of unexplained UFO phenomena (sightings, abductions, etc.). The Bible says that prior to the return of the Lord Jesus Christ that it will be just like it was in the days of Noah. Is it possible that the "sons of God" are on yet another collision course with the inhabitants of Earth? Are we even now witnessing the opening scenario? What does the Bible have to say about this future invasion? In the following chapters we will discover that the Bible has much to say about the ET (extraterrestrial or end-times) invasion of planet Earth.

Chapter Nine

The eX– Files

More and more we are finding that mythology in general, though greatly contorted, very often has some historic base. And the interesting thing is that one myth which occurs over and over again in many parts of the world is that somewhere a long time ago supernatural beings had sexual intercourse with natural women and produced a special breed of people.

—Francis A. Schaeffer

I think you will agree that Genesis 6:1–4 is a mysterious, yet amazing portion of God's Word. The entire notion of angelic beings taking on human flesh, marrying human wives, procreating, and producing a mongrel race of beings is strange to say the least.

But someone might be thinking at this point, "Is there any other evidence outside the pages of the Bible that sub-

UFO photographed by Hannah McRoberts in October 1981. She was photographing the mountain, and neither she nor her companions saw the UFO. Location: north of Kelsey Bay, Vancouver Island, British Columbia, Canada.

stantiates such an unbelievable event? Certainly if such a monumental event occurred in human history there would be other records of it outside the Bible."

Interestingly, there are other ancient, extra-biblical documents that recount the presence of fallen angels in the affairs of men just as described in Genesis 6. In this chapter we want to cite this extra-biblical support for the view we have adopted of Genesis 6. We call these documents the *eX*–files.

An Ancient Best Seller

The first document in the eX-files that relates to this subject is the mysterious Book of Enoch which was written over a period of time by several writers. Most of the work was probably done between 200–100 B.C.

While this document was not known in Europe until the eighteenth century, it was a veritable best seller in the first century. According to many experts, it was probably the most influential apocalyptic work outside the canonical Scriptures. Tertullian and some of the other early church fathers considered it of such import that they included it as part of the Scripture.

The book of Jude in the New Testament in verses 14–15 quotes directly from Enoch 1:9; 5:4; and 27:2.

The book of Enoch is important for our purposes in that it speaks extensively of the "sons of God" or "Watchers" (a term also found in Daniel 4:13, 17, and 23) who came to Earth and cohabited with women. It provides extensive details not found in the Genesis record but that do not contradict the account in Genesis.

Enoch refers to the *grogori,* or "fallen angels," who broke their vows, married the daughters of men, and "befouled the earth with their deeds." He also mentions the product of these unions as "giants."

The Book of Enoch alleges that two hundred of these watchers descended in the days of Jared (Gen. 5:18) to the summit of Mount Hermon. Seventeen of them are given names and are spoken of as "their chiefs of tens" (Enoch 6:8). The most wicked of them all was their leader Azaz'el.

Here are a few selected passages from Enoch to show how it corroborates the Genesis account.

> In those days, when the children of man had multiplied, it happened that there were born unto them handsome and beautiful daughters. And the angels, the children of heaven, saw them and desired them; and they said to one another, "Come let us choose wives for ourselves from among the daughters of man and beget us children."
>
> —see Gen. 6:1–2

> And they took wives unto themselves, and everyone [respectively] chose one woman for himself, and they began to go unto them. And they taught them magical medicine, incantations, the cutting of roots, and taught them about plants. And the women became pregnant and gave birth to great giants whose heights were three hundred cubits. These giants consumed the produce of all the people until the people detested feeding them. So the giants turned against the people in order to eat them. And they began to sin against birds, wild beasts, reptiles, and fish. And their flesh was devoured the one by the other, and they drank blood. And then the earth brought an accusation against the oppressors.
>
> —see Gen. 7:1–6

Because of the debauchery, Enoch is called by God to issue a warning to the Watchers.

> Enoch, scribe of righteousness, go and make known to the Watchers of heaven who have abandoned the high heaven, the holy eternal place, and have defiled themselves with

women, as their deeds move the children of the world, and
have taken unto themselves wives: They have defiled themselves with great defilement upon the earth; neither will
there be peace unto them nor the forgiveness of sin

—see Gen. 12:4–6

The Book of Enoch even gives us the means by which this
information was collected, preserved, and transmitted.
Enoch's son Methusaleh was to preserve this information and
hand it down to the coming generations of the world.

The Book of Enoch powerfully confirms the biblical record
in Genesis 6 that the Earth was visited, defiled, and polluted
by an incursion of extraterrestrial beings in the days before
the flood.

Jubilees

The Book of Jubilees is a fifty-chapter book which was originally written in Hebrew between 161–140 B.C. While it cov-
ers many subjects, it is important for the subject at hand because of its introduction of a host of angels and demons, especially a class of angels known as the Watchers. According
to Jubilees these Watchers were sent to Earth to instruct men
and to do righteousness (4:15) but they corrupted themselves
by having intercourse with the daughters of men who bore
them giants (4:21–23; 7:21f.). The Watchers also fathered a
host of evil demons who plagued the sons of Noah (10:10–6).
God sent the flood in order to destroy the Earth.

For on account of these three the flood came upon the earth.
For it was because of the fornication which the Watchers,
apart from the mandate of their authority, fornicated with
the daughters of men and took for themselves wives from
all whom they chose and made a beginning of impurity. And
they begot sons, the Naphidim, and all of them were dis-

similar. And each one ate his fellow.

176

her inf...
from th...

Jubilees adds a few more details '
angelic visitation of Earth. It rev.
Watchers descended to Earth as 461 ..
has been interpreted as 3543 B.C. It also notes ..
ers were especially associated with Jared, the fiftn .
Adam. "And he called his name Jared for in his days .
gels of the Lord descended on the earth, those so named ..
Watchers" (4:15).

Jubilees reveals to us that the Watchers were originally
good angels (4:15) who fell into sin with the daughters of
men and were bound in the midst of the Earth (5:6–11). Their
children, the giants, were destroyed, but the spirits of their
children wander the Earth as demons, causing diseases
(10:11f.), leading men astray (10:1f.), seeking human sacri-
fice, and encouraging idolatry (1:11).

This overall picture is certainly consistent with the description of what happened in Genesis 6.

The Dead Sea Scrolls

Among the discovered documents and fragments near
Qumran among the Dead Sea Scrolls are two more ancient
documents that corroborate the Genesis 6 account.

The first is the Genesis Apocryphon (sometimes called
the Lamech Scroll). This document relates the story of Lamech
(Gen. 4:18–24) who had been away on a far journey from
home. When he finally returns, he discovers that his wife
Bitenosh had given birth to a boy in his absence. He was certain that the child was not his and the child bore no resemblance to anyone in his family. Compounding the mystery
was the fact that the boy was exceedingly beautiful, and when
he opened his eyes he lit up the whole house. Lamech did
what most husbands would do—he confronted his wife with

...elity, but he thought that the child was conceived ...e Watchers and was one of the Nephilim.

> Behold, then, I thought in my heart that the conception was
> the work of the Watchers and the pregnancy, of the Holy
> Ones, and it belonged to the Giants and my heart within
> me was upset on account of this boy. Then I, Lamech, was
> frightened and turned to Bitenosh, my wife, and said, Swear
> to me by the Most High, by the Great Lord, by the King of
> the Universe, the sons of heaven, that you will in truth let
> me know everything. . . Then Bitenosh, my bride, spoke to
> me very harshly, she wept and said: Oh my brother and lord
> . . . I swear to you . . . that this seed comes from you, and not
> from any foreigner or watcher or son of heaven.

Lamech, a descendant of Cain, evidently believed that it was possible that his son could have been conceived by a Watcher or heavenly being.

Another fragment in the Dead Sea Scrolls is called the Book of Giants. While this document is very fragmented, there is enough material present to gather that it is speaking about defilement, the giants and nephilim, their incredible power, their bloodthirstiness and their ultimate destruction by God.

Folklore and Fables

As you can see, the evidence for the extraterrestrial invasion of Earth in Genesis 6 and existence of the nephilim goes far beyond the biblical record. Many ancient documents cite the same occurrence, only with more detailed descriptions. In fact, one could say that all of ancient mythology in Sumer, Egypt, Babylon, Assyria, Persia, Greece, and Rome is based on this same fundamental notion of the "gods" coming down and siring children with human women. Most people are at least vaguely acquainted with the mythologies of ancient Greece and Rome. The gods have different names such as Zeus or

Jupiter, Poseidon or Neptune, Aphrodite or Venus, Eros or Cupid, but their sex orgies and promiscuities are all the same and so are their offspring.

Homer's classic, *The Odyssey,* was recently adapted for television and was shown in a two-part series. One of the main theses of the movie was the fact that the demigods had children by human women and created a super-race of beings.

In the Sumerian culture, the oldest known civilization with a written language, the hero of one of their epics is a man named Gilgamesh, who is described as two-thirds god and one-third man. He was a god-man—the product of a divine–human sexual relationship.

As Francis A. Schaeffer wrote:

> More and more we are finding that mythology in general, though greatly contorted, very often has some historic base. And the interesting thing is that one myth which occurs over and over again in many parts of the world is that somewhere a long time ago supernatural beings had sexual intercourse with natural women and produced a special breed of people.

Probably the best known tale of the ancient gods is that of Zeus, whose lust knew no boundaries as numerous women were seduced by him including Thetis, Europa, Leda, Metis, and Dione. As Emil Gaverluk says in his book *Did Genesis Man Conquer Space?*:

> Zeus' amorous victories illustrate the actions of uncontrolled spirit-beings lusting after human flesh. The whole story of Greek mythology is an expanded version of that astonishing verse in the Bible: "The sons of God saw the daughters of men that they were fair; and they took them wives of all which they chose" (Gen. 6:2). The mythology of the past is

a startling revelation of the uncontrolled behavior of both spirit-beings and rebellious man.

"Engage"

It seems clear, therefore, from both the Bible and the eX-files that extraterrestrial, demonic beings did invade Earth in the days before the flood judgment. The Earth has experienced at least one "extraterrestrial" invasion in the past, but what about the future? Is it possible that there could be another invasion in the future? Will these extraterrestrial beings come to Earth again?

One of my favorite lines in *Star Trek: The Next Generation* is when Captain Picard sits on the bridge of the *Starship Enterprise,* sets the coordinates for the next destination, gives the command for the appropriate warp setting, and then dramatically raises his left hand, points forward, and says, "Engage"!

Well, we are about to engage at warp speed to the end times, so fasten your spiritual seat belt as we move from Genesis to Revelation—from the beginning of time to the end of time!

Chapter Ten

ET: Extraterrestrials
or End Times?

*But as the days of Noe were, so shall also
the coming of the Son of man be. For as in
the days that were before the flood they
were eating and drinking, marrying and
giving in marriage, until the day that Noe
entered into the ark, And knew not until
the flood came, and took them all away;
so shall also the coming of the Son of man
be.*

—Matthew 24:37–39

Since 1993 the UFO Festival has been an annual event in Roswell, New Mexico. In July 1996 the festival drew twelve thousand visitors. During the week of July 1–6, 1997, 150,000 people descended on the quiet city of Roswell, New Mexico, to celebrate and memorialize the fiftieth anniversary of the original Roswell incident in July 1947.

All one thousand hotel rooms in Roswell were booked by February, and most hotels within a ninety-mile radius of Roswell were booked up. Organizers also cleared several acres for campers and RVs. The chief draw of the festival was a really alternative rock concert watched by millions on the Fox network as part of a week of alien mania.

The UFO Museum and Research Center in Roswell had 69,000 people pass through its doors in 1996, twice as many as in 1995, necessitating a move from a 3,000-square-foot office to a 12,000-square-foot renovated movie theater.

People are focused on the UFO craze with an overpowering urge to know. Many view this as a sign of the last days. With the incredible proliferation of UFOs in our culture, one key question that "enquiring minds want to know" about UFOs is: Could this be a signal of the beginning of the end times? Are UFOs an eschatological sign of the the last days? Especially with the year 2000 rapidly approaching, people have an ominous sense that UFOs portend that the end is near.

While no one can say for certain, there do seem to be several factors that suggest that the modern UFO explosion is no accident. Let's look at two of these factors together.

The Importance of 1948

In many ways 1948 was the most momentous year for Christians since Pentecost in Jerusalem nearly two thousand years ago. Several beginnings occurred that year that seem to mark it as a key year in the final unfolding of the end of the age. Consider these events that all converged in this one year.

1. **The National Council of Churches** was formed with the hope that this organization would one day usher in a one-world church. The hope was that by uniting many churches, the differences and disagreements would disappear and peace would be possible. This event is significant because the Bible predicts that in the last days all the world will be united in a great one-world religion where all men on Earth will worship a man as God (2 Thess. 2:4; Rev. 13:8,15).

2. **The European Common Market** came into being at the Hague Congress in 1948. This union was the precursor to the present European Union that is bringing Europe back together again, just as the Bible predicted twenty-six hundred years ago with the prophet Daniel. In Daniel 2:40–44; 7:7,17–24 and in Revelation 13:1– 2 and 17:8–12, the Bible states that in the last days the Roman Empire will be reunited in a ten-nation (kingdom) form or confederation. In Daniel 2 it is pictured by ten toes on Nebuchadnezzar's statue, and in Daniel 7, Revelation 13 and 17, by ten horns on a horrible beast. This ten-nation confederation represents the reunited or last days form of the Roman Empire that will be the ruling world power when Jesus Christ returns to establish His kingdom on Earth. The beginning of the reuniting of Europe occurred in 1948 and is rapidly progressing toward consummation.

3. **The re-establishment of the State of Israel.** At 4:00 p.m. on May 14, 1948, David Ben Gurion banged the table in Tel Aviv and announced to the world the establishment of the Jewish state called Israel. Then he added, "The Bible is our mandate." Eleven minutes later, President Harry Truman officially recognized

the State of Israel. The importance of this event in Bible prophecy cannot be overemphasized. All of the prophecies in the Bible regarding the last days presuppose that Israel is a nation gathered back into her land (see Isa. 11:11–12; Ezek. 37). Once again, 1948 was the key year for the beginning of the regathering of the Jewish people into the Promised Land.

4. **The discovery of the Dead Sea Scrolls** in November 1947 became known to the world in 1948. These ancient scrolls and fragments contain some of the most important finds in the history of biblical archaeology.

5. **The space age** began in 1948 when experiments with liquid hydrogen proved that a rocket could be sent into space beyond the gravitational pull of Earth.

6. **The birth of ufology** began in 1947–48 when strange objects began to appear on Earth. The modern UFO era began fifty years ago on June 24, 1947, when Kenneth Arnold was piloting his plane through the crystal clear skies around the Cascade Mountains in Washington State. He saw nine crescent-shaped discs and reported that they were "like saucers skipping across the water." Not long after this, the phrase "flying saucer" entered the American vocabulary.

One month later on July 4, 1947, the now-famous Roswell incident occurred. This event has become the capstone in the arch of the modern UFO movement.

Since 1947–48 thousands of UFOs have been reported around the world. Fifty years have passed and the UFO mystery has survived and even strengthened. Make no mistake, UFOs are here to stay.

While no one can say for certain that the "last days" or the "end times" began in 1948, it is interesting how so many key events, some of which are mentioned in Bible prophecy, trace their genesis to this one year.

Aliens from the Abyss

All of the current UFO mania could very well be a time of preparation for the world's last-days alien invasion of planet Earth. In the Book of Revelation, God's Word predicts an invasion of this Earth by beings from another sphere. It will be an all-out invasion of planet Earth resulting in massive destruction and the death of billions of people. We firmly believe that many of the recent disaster movies focusing on tornadoes, volcanos, and all-out alien invasions are preparing the minds of people for the last days disasters of the coming Tribulation period. The focus on these phenomena, especially UFOs and the paranormal, are preparing people to accept anything. When the Rapture of the Church occurs and millions of believers immediately disappear, how will the world explain it? We can't say for sure, but it is possible there will be some UFO, paranormal, or New Age explanation. All the focus on disasters, aliens, and the paranormal, play heavily on the theme of Judgment Day eschatology. People seem to be expecting some great event to occur, especially in light of the coming of A.D. 2000.

Regardless of the relationship of the current craze to the end of the age, it is certain that the last days will unfold exactly as the Word of God has predicted. And one of the judgments of the Tribulation period is an "alien" invasion of planet Earth—an alien invasion of unimaginable scope and severity. In light of all the attention aliens are receiving today, we need to understand what the Bible says about this end-time invasion of planet Earth. We need to answer several key questions about this invasion, such as: Who are these last days alien invaders? Where do they come from? What do they look like? Why do they come to Earth? Is there any hope for the planet?

The next four chapters will answer these questions and more!

Chapter Eleven

Close Encounters
of the Seventh Kind

And I saw an angel come down from heaven, having the key of the bottomless pit and a great chain in his hand. And he laid hold on the dragon, that old serpent, which is the Devil, and Satan, and bound him a thousand years, And cast him into the bottomless pit, and shut him up, and set a seal upon him, that he should deceive the nations no more, till the thousand years should be fulfilled: and after that he must be loosed a little season.

—Rev 20:1-3

The science of ufology specifies six distinct categories of sightings:

1. **Close Encounters of the First Kind.** This refers to mere sighting of an unidentified flying object at close quarters.
2. **Close Encounters of the Second Kind.** This includes not only sightings of a UFO at close quarters, but the presence of certain physical records of the craft having been there. These records may be tangible marks on the ground, the scorching of grass, crop circles, interference with electrical circuits, or physical effects on animals or humans such as temporary paralysis or weightlessness.
3. **Close Encounters of the Third Kind.** This is even more bizarre and incredible than the first two because it includes, in addition to the two distinctives above, a direct confrontation with an alien or space-being, often referred to as a humanoid.
4. **Close Encounters of the Fourth Kind.** The next category of alien contact is reserved for an even more startling encounter—abduction by aliens.
5. **Close Encounters of the Fifth Kind.** This level of encounter involves contact with alien life forms through metaphysical means, that is, personal contact with UFO entities through metaphysical or other occult means.
6. **Close Encounter of the Sixth Kind.** The final category of alien encounter is the most serious of all—injury or death from a UFO encounter.

As we have already seen, the first book of the Bible (Genesis) describes an alien encounter that goes beyond any of the categories of sightings man has developed—alien beings penetrating the earthly sphere and intermarrying with human women.

In the last book of the Bible (Revelation) another alien invasion is revealed that will occur in the last days. Revelation 9 describes contact with alien beings unlike anything that man has ever experienced. There is no present category of UFO sighting that fits what the Bible reveals will occur. Revelation 9 describes an all-out invasion of Earth by alien beings from another world, another sphere, another universe—an alien invasion where the mask comes off and the true nature of these beings is revealed. It's what I want to refer to as *a close encounter of the seventh kind.*

Three Terrible Trumpets

Before considering some of the facts in Revelation 9, it's important to get our bearings with a brief overview of Bible prophecy and the book of Revelation. The next major event on God's prophetic timetable is the Rapture of the Church when all dead Church age believers will be resurrected with glorified bodies, and all living believers will be immediately translated into the presence of the Lord. First Thessalonians 4:15–18 describes this glorious event.

> For this we say unto you by the word of the Lord, that we which are alive and remain unto the coming of the Lord shall not prevent them which are asleep. For the Lord himself shall descend from heaven with a shout, with the voice of the archangel, and with the trump of God: and the dead in Christ shall rise first: Then we which are alive and remain shall be caught up together with them in the clouds, to meet the Lord in the air: and so shall we ever be with the Lord. Wherefore comfort one another with these words.

Sometime after the Rapture of the Church a seven-year period of time will be inaugurated when the Antichrist makes a treaty with the people of Israel (Dan. 9:27). This seven-year period is known as "the seventieth week of Daniel," "the tribulation period" (Matt. 24:9,29), "the time of Jacob's trouble" (Jer. 30:7), "the indignation" (Isa. 26:20–21), "a time of trouble such as never was" (Dan. 12:1). This period of time is described in detail from commencement to consummation in Revelation 6–19. The main sections in Revelation 6–19 are three series of seven judgments poured out by God on the Earth and its inhabitants: seven seals, seven trumpets, and seven bowls of wrath.

When one reaches Revelation 8:1–2 the seven seal judgments have already been opened, with the final seal containing the seven trumpets. In Revelation 8:6–12 the first four trumpets are blown, wreaking their havoc on the Earth and affecting one-third of the Earth, the trees, the green grass, the sea, the creatures in the sea, the ships, the fresh water, the sun, the moon, and the stars.

Revelation 8:13 is the climax. John sees an angel flying in the mid-heaven crying out, "Woe, woe, woe, to the inhabiters of the earth by reason of the other voices of the trumpet of the three angels, which are yet to sound!" The final three trumpets are called three "woes" or calamities. It is an interjection denoting pain, an exclamation of a thing concerning which pain is expressed.

I've never heard an angel, but John did, and the message was not a positive one. This talking angel is announcing the coming of piercing, intensified pain upon the entire unbelieving world. The final three trumpet judgments are singled out as much worse than the first four, because now the judgments involve people as their objects.

A Falling Star

When the fifth angel sounds his trumpet in Revelation 9:1 the first woe is unleashed, and the first thing John sees is "a star fall from heaven unto the earth." The star he sees is not a literal star as in 6:13 and 8:10,12, but rather a fallen angel. We know that the star represents a person because the key to the bottomles pit is given to him. A key cannot be given to a literal star. Moreover, in Revelation 1:20 stars are symbols of angels (see also Job 38:7). Since this angel has fallen to the Earth, he must be either a fallen angel or Satan. The word "fall" denotes past completed action in Greek. It seems better to see this angel, mentioned here almost in passing, as one of the evil, fallen angels dispatched by God to advance the next stage of His judgment against the rebellious Earth-dwellers by opening the bottomless pit.

God alone retains permanent possession of the key to the bottomless pit, but He gives it temporarily to this fallen angel to accomplish His sovereign purposes. He is in control! What a comfort that should be to us.

The Black Hole

Beginning in Revelation 9:1 there are three references in this chapter to the "bottomless pit" or, literally, "the shaft of the abyss" (vv. 1,2,11). The word *abussos,* or "abyss," is found nine times in the New Testament, with seven of the references in the book of Revelation (Luke 8:31; Rom.10:7; Rev. 9:1,2,11; 11:7; 17:8; 20:1,3).

In the New Testmament, four parts of the underworld, or netherworld, are delineated: Gehenna (the lake of fire), Hades, Tartarus, and the Abyss.

Gehenna, which is also called the lake of fire or the lake of burning sulphur, is referred to twelve times in the New Testament. Amazingly, eleven of the twelve references are found on the lips of our Savior, the Lord Jesus Christ. The word *Gehenna* is the Greek equivalent for "the Valley of Hinnom." Robert Morey (*Death and the Afterlife,* 87) describes the Valley of Hinnom.

The word Gehenna is the Greek equivalent for the Valley

of Hinnom. It thus originally referred to the Valley of Hinnom, which was just outside the city of Jerusalem. According to *Thayer's Greek-English Lexicon* it was the place where idolatrous Jews gave human sacrifices to pagan deities. Because of these horrible idolatrous practices, the Valley of Hinnom was hated and considered unclean by pious Jews. In Christ's day this hatred of the Valley of Hinnom caused the valley to become the town dump where all the garbage of Jerusalem could be thrown. Unclean corpses, as well as normal garbage, were thrown into it. Because garbage was constantly being thrown into the valley, the fires never stopped burning, and the worms never stopped eating.

The Valley of Hinnom was the place where worms devoured rotting flesh. It was used as the burial place for criminals and burning garbage. Jesus used this as the background and picture for the final, eternal destiny of the lost.

Consider the following frightening facts about Gehenna.

1. Gehenna, or the lake of fire, is the final place of punishment for all unsaved men, fallen angels, and Satan (Rev. 20:10–15).
2. Gehenna is a place of conscious torment of both the body and the soul (Matt. 10:28).
3. Gehenna is a place of eternal, never-ending torment. It will last forever! (Matt. 25:46; 2 Thess. 1:9; Rev. 14:11).
4. Gehenna is a place of unquenchable fire (Mark 9:45); a place of never-dying worms (Mark 9:46); a lake of burning sulphur (Rev. 20:14); the blackness of darkness forever (Jude 1:13); a place of separation from God (2 Thess. 1:9); a place of outer darkness (Matt. 8:12); a place of weeping and gnashing of teeth (Matt. 8:12).

While Gehenna is the final destiny of all the lost, Hades is the *present* place of imprisonment for the disembodied spirits of lost men. The word Hades is found ten times in the New Testament. The clearest description of Hades is found in Luke 16:19–31 where the rich man died and went to Hades where he was tormented. This passage reveals to us that Hades is a place of conscious torment from which there is no relief and no escape. Luke 16:26 says: "And beside all this, between us and you there is a great gulf fixed: so that they which would pass from hence to you cannot; neither can they pass to us, that would come from thence."

However, Hades is only a *temporary* place of confinement for the spirits of lost men. The bodies of the lost will one day be resurrected and reunited with their spirits, and they will be judged at the Great White Throne judgment and cast into Gehenna, or the lake of fire. Revelation 20:13–15 describes this awful, mind-numbing scene:

> And the sea gave up the dead which were in it; and death and hell delivered up the dead which were in them: and they were judged every man according to their works. And death and hell were cast into the lake of fire. This is the second death. And whosoever was not found written in the book of life was cast into the lake of fire.

This passage reveals that Hades is a place of temporary torment for the souls of lost men. When an unbeliever dies, his immaterial part immediately goes to Hades, while his body sleeps in the grave. After the millennial reign of Christ described in Revelation 20:1–6, the bodies of the lost will be resurrected, they will be judged and then permanently cast, body and soul, into the lake of fire to endure everlasting judgment at the hands of a righteous, holy God. As some have described it, Hades is like a county jail where one is held temporarily, and Gehenna is like the penitentiary, the final place of judgment.

The third part of the underworld, called Tartarus, is only mentioned by name in one place in the New Testament—2 Peter 2:4. It is the permament abode of the fallen angels who sinned in Genesis 6:1–4 until the final judgment when they are cast into the lake of fire. Second Peter 2:4 says: "For if God spared not the angels that sinned, but cast them down to hell [literally, Tartarus], and delivered them into chains of darkness, to be reserved unto judgment." Jude 6–7 is a parallel passage to 2 Peter 2:4 and describes what these angels did to be consigned to Tartarus.

> And the angels which kept not their first estate, but left their own habitation, he hath reserved in everlasting chains under darkness unto the judgment of the great day. Even as Sodom and Gomorrha, and the cities about them in like manner, giving themselves over to fornication, and going after strange flesh, are set forth for an example, suffering the vengeance of eternal fire.
>
> —Jude 6–7

Tartarus is the special place of judgment for these fallen angels in Genesis 6:1–4 who went too far in their rebellion, left their own domain, and plunged into gross immorality by seducing human women.

The final part of the netherworld, and the one that is most relevant to Revelation 9, is called the abyss or, literally, "the shaft of the abyss." The Greek word *abussos* appears nine times in the New Testament (Luke 8:31; Rom. 10:7; Rev. 9:1,2,11; 11:7; 17:8; 20:1,3). The shaft of the abyss pictures a subterranean cavern connected to the Earth's surface by a shaft or well whose opening has a sealed lid of some type.

In Luke 8:30–32, the legion of demons in the Gadarene demoniac begged Jesus to allow them to inhabit the bodies of some nearby pigs and not to send them to the abyss before the time. Jesus allows them to enter the swine and the swine rush down the bank into the lake and drown. This was the original "Bay of Pigs" incident!

Revelation 17:8 says that the Antichrist, the coming world ruler, ascends from the abyss.

> The beast that thou sawest was, and is not; and shall ascend out of the bottomless pit, and go into perdition: and they that dwell on the earth shall wonder, whose names were not written in the book of life from the foundation of the world, when they behold the beast that was, and is not, and yet is (see also, Rev 11:7).

Taking these verses with Revelation 13:3,12,14 reveals that the Beast or Antichrist will suffer some sort of fatal wound from which he will return to life. When he does return, "he will come back in a demonic rather than a purely human form to establish his world domination" (Thomas, *Revelation*, 2:294). The Antichrist will arise from the abyss and be entirely empowered and energized by Satan (see Rev. 13:4–5).

Revelation 20 states that Satan will be cast into the abyss and bound there for one thousand years while Christ rules and reigns on Earth.

> And I saw an angel come down from heaven, having the key of the bottomless pit and a great chain in his hand. And he laid hold on the dragon, that old serpent, which is the Devil, and Satan, and bound him a thousand years, And cast him into the bottomless pit, and shut him up, and set a seal upon him, that he should deceive the nations no more, till the thousand years should be fulfilled: and after that he must be loosed a little season.
>
> —Rev 20:1–3

The shaft of the abyss is a place of *temporary* confinement for some of the fallen angels or demons. When the fifth angel sounds his trumpet, the star from heaven is given the key to the abyss and opens its dark door for the first time we know of in man's history.

Dark Skies

Several years ago I (Mark) took my family to visit Carlsbad Caverns in New Mexico. I can still feel our slow descent into the bowels of the Earth and still smell the musty air of the caverns. The trip is an exciting adventure from start to finish. But the highlight of the trip is the flight of the bats from the cave at dusk when bats begin their nightly exodus to feed on the insects in the surrounding area. As the thousands of bats fly out of the hole in the Earth the little light that remains at dusk is darkened by their flight. The scene is awesome in its beauty and uniqueness.

In a much more vivid and frightening scene, Revelation 9:2–3 describes the opening of the abyss, the release of smoke of a great furnace, and myriads of locustlike beings swarming out on the Earth as the shaft of the abyss belches forth smoke and locusts that darken the skies of the entire Earth. Smoke billows forth from this prison house of wickedness, and these locusts ooze from the abyss. As H. A. Ironside says: "It is quite difficult to express the effect produced by the sight of the whole atmosphere filled on all sides and to a great height by an innumerable quantity of these insects, whose flight was slow and uniform and whose noise that of rain" (Ironside, *Revelation*, 157).

But what or who comes forth from this subterranean pit to block the rays of the sun? Who are these locusts that swarm out of the abyss and darken the skies of the Earth? Are they literal locusts or some other creatures?

The Soot of Hell

The locusts in Revelation 9 have been interpreted at different times in church history to symbolize heretics, the Goths, the Mohammedans, the mendicant orders, the Jesuits, the Protestants, the Saracens, and the Turks. However, the description in Revelation 9:2–5 reveals that these locusts are demonic beings in material, visible form. They are the uncanny denizens of the abyss, locusts of a hellish species animated with infernal powers. This passage describes an unbelievable demonic invasion of Earth by Satan's war corps in the last days.

There are six factors that support the view that these beings are demons in material form. First, as we have already seen in verse one, their leader is a fallen angel or demon.

Second, they come from the shaft of the abyss, which in the New Testament is consistently the place where some fallen angels or demons are consigned (Luke 8:31). The abyss is the place where Satan will be confined for one thousand years during the millennial reign of Christ (Rev. 20:1–3).

Third, they cannot be literal locusts because their object of attack is people, not vegetation. Revelation 9:4 says: "And it was commanded them that they should not hurt the grass of the earth, neither any green thing, neither any tree; but only those men which have not the seal of God in their foreheads." Literal locusts strip vegetation and leave people alone. These locusts do just the opposite.

Fourth, these locusts only torture those who do not belong to God. This is consistent with the activity of demons.

Fifth, demons have the apparent ability to appear in an assortment of material forms, both human and animal. In Revelation 16:13 demons appear as unclean frogs.

Sixth, the description of these beings in Revelation 9:7–10 clearly goes far beyond anything from this world.

Seventh, literal locusts have no king over them. Proverbs 30:27 says, "The locusts have no king, yet go they forth all of them by bands." The locusts described in this passage have the "angel of the bottomless pit" as their leader (Rev 9:11). These are demonic beings in material form led forth by their king, "the angel of the bottomless pit."

John MacArthur, Jr., agrees with this conclusion.

What are the locusts of Revelation 9:1–12?

I believe that the locusts that come out of the bottomless pit during the fifth trumpet judgment of the Tribulation (Rev. 9:1–12) are demons. Now I know that these locusts have been interpreted as referring to Moslems, or
helicopters, or whatever else; but I believe they are clearly
demons. Why? Because it says that these locusts originated
from the bottomless pit after it was unlocked. And the only
things locked in the bottomless pit (*abussos*) are demons.

In the ancient world there was nothing more destructive than
locusts. They were symbolic of destruction. The fifth trumpet judgment of the last days describes nothing less than the
bowels of hell belching forth a horrid host of foul, fiendish
demons to afflict unsaved people with excruciating pain and
torture in the last days of the coming Tribulation period.

God's Early Release Program

Prison overcrowding has become a chronic problem in the
Oklahoma Department of Corrections (our home state) and
in probably every other state as well. To alleviate the overcrowding, many solutions have been suggested. The most con-
troversial in recent months has been the early release program for "non-violent" offenders. The controversy escalated
when an inmate incarcerated for a non-violent offense was
released from the penitentiary early and within a few hours
killed his ex-wife and her parents. Upon further investigation
officials discovered that while his most recent offense was non-
violent, he had a long list of prior convictions for violent
crimes. The system had failed. This one raging man murdered
three people within hours of his release.

Picture what the world would be like if the doors of the

jails and penitentiaries of the Earth were opened and the world's most vicious and violent criminals were set free, giving them full reign to practice their mayhem and infamies upon mankind. The scene in Revelation 9 is much, much worse. What will it be like when countless thousands of demons who have been chained in the abyss for thousands of years run rampant throughout the Earth in visible form during this time of the Tribulation? It will be unspeakable!

Add to this the fact that in Revelation 12 Satan and his fallen host are cast down from heaven to the Earth. The Earth will be caught in the demonic crossfire as Satan and the fallen angels are cast from the atmospheric, stellar, and divine heavens above down to the Earth, and the demons from the abyss below are dredged up to the Earth. The Earth will literally be teeming with swarms of dreadful demonic beings. It will be an Auschwitz type of experience for those who must endure it. The diabolical forces from both heaven and hell will be unleashed to practice their indescribable, unimaginable atrocities upon mankind.

Of course, this bizarre scenario raises all kinds of questions, many of which we cannot answer. But Revelation 9 answers at least three important questions that inquiring minds want to know: 1) What will these beings look like? 2) What will they do to the people on the Earth? and 3) Are there any limitations to their destruction?

The next chapter answers these key questions.

Chapter Twelve

War of the Worlds

And the shapes of the locusts were like unto horses prepared unto battle; and on their heads were as it were crowns like gold, and their faces were as the faces of men. And they had hair as the hair of women, and their teeth were as the teeth of lions. And they had breastplates, as it were breast-plates of iron; and the sound of their wings was as the sound of chariots of many horses running to battle. And they had tails like unto scorpions, and there were stings in their tails: and their power was to hurt men five months.

—Rev. 9: 7–10

On October 30, 1938, Orson Welles and the Mercury Theatre of the Air presented—in the form of a news bulletin—a radio adaptation of H. G. Wells' novella *War of the Worlds* over the Columbia Broadcasting System. Between eight and nine o'clock eastern standard time music programming was seemingly interrupted by fictional commentator Carl Phillips who announced that creatures from Mars had landed in New Jersey and were on the attack. Before Welles could close the program and assure listeners that what they were hearing was only "the Mercury Theatre's own radio version of dressing up in a sheet and jumping out of a bush and saying, Boo!" the nation panicked.

It is estimated that 6 million people heard the broadcast on the eve of Halloween and 1.2 million took it literally. Hundreds of cars streamed from the cities mentioned in the broadcast and several suicide attempts were reported. Most people who took it literally huddled before windows watching and waiting for the worst.

One of the most interesting phenomena was that reports began to flood in from people claiming to see the attack. Some swore they saw patches of fire consuming isolated portions of the countryside. Others described seeing huge metal cylinders plummeting heavily toward Earth. Several confused people in New Jersey warned police that Martians on their three-legged war machines were perched on the Jersey Palisades preparing to cross the Hudson and seize New York City.

Many since that time have wondered how otherwise rational people could react with such panic and cower before their own imaginations. In his book *Invasion from Mars* Professor Hadley Cantril of Princeton University believed that the timing of the broadcast helps explain the panic and hallucinations. The broadcast was sandwiched between the Great

Depression and the coming war when Americans were extremely anxious and in anticipation of something monumental.

As the millennium approaches, there is once again a powerful sense of anticipation and anxiety in our world—the sense that some monumental milestone is on the horizon. People today are even more primed for a "war of the worlds" event than they were in 1938. In fact, many people are confidently expecting an invasion from beyond. And amazingly, this is exactly what the Bible predicts in the last days.

Revelation 9 reveals that in the last days of planet Earth, known as the Tribulation period, the Earth will be invaded by a force of "aliens" unlike anything man could ever concoct in a special effects lab. This invasion will make *War of the Worlds* look like a Sunday school picnic.

Let's see what Revelation says about these beings from below that will invade our planet in the last days.

Who's in Control?

At the very beginning of the description of what these beings look like and what they do, God makes it crystal clear that He is in total control. He gives the key to the abyss to the fallen angel and He places strict limitations on each and every movement.

God places at least three strict limitations on what these beings can do in Revelation 9:4–5: who they can strike, how they can strike, and how long they can strike.

Who they can strike

As these demonic hordes overrun the Earth, God expressly forbids them to harm "the grass of the earth, neither any green thing, neither any tree; but only those men which have not the seal of God in their foreheads" (v. 4) They cannot harm grass, plants, trees, or believers in Jesus Christ. Those with the seal of God in their foreheads are mentioned in Revelation 7:4–8. They are the 144,000 who are exempt from the demonic torture. While they are certainly secure from this plague, this limitation will probably also include all believers in the Earth at that time.

Now I know that some of you are probably asking yourself, "I thought you said earlier that all believers will be raptured before the Tribulation period begins. Who are these believers on the Earth that are delivered from this demon plague?"

We must remember that many people will be brought to a saving knowledge of Jesus Christ during the Tribulation period. Revelation 7 mentions at least two groups of people who will be saved during the Tribulation period: the 144,00 Jews and a great multitude of Gentiles.

Revelation 7:9,13–14 says:

> After this I beheld, and, lo, a great multitude, which no man could number, of all nations, and kindreds, and people, and tongues, stood before the throne, and before the Lamb, clothed with white robes, and palms in their hands; . . . And one of the elders answered, saying unto me, What are these which are arrayed in white robes? and whence came they? And I said unto him, Sir, thou knowest. And he said to me, These are they which came out of great tribulation, and have washed their robes, and made them white in the blood of the Lamb.

God will use the turbulent time of the Tribulation to call many lost sinners to Himself for salvation. While many of them will suffer persecution and even martyrdom during the Tribulation, they will be divinely spared from the evil effects of the fifth trumpet and the foul demons who torment the lost.

This same pattern of divine protection can be observed in the book of Exodus during the plagues on Pharoah and Egypt. When God poured the ten plagues on the Egyptians to bring

Pharaoh to his knees, God's people were spared from their evil effects (Exod. 8:22–23; 9:4,6,26; 10:23). It's interesting how many of the Egyptian plagues are paralleled in Revelation.

Exodus	Revelation
Water turned to blood (7:14-25)	8:8; 11:6; 16:3
Frogs (8:1–15)	16:13
Boils (9:8–11)	16:2
Hail (9:18–33)	8:7; 16:21
Locusts (10:1–19)	9:1–10
Darkness (10:21–26)	8:12; 16:10

The eighth Egyptian plague was a plague of literal locusts that covered the land of Egypt. Frequently in the Bible, locusts are used by the Lord as a divine judgment on the wicked world (cf. Joel 1:4–7). The fifth trumpet in Revelation is a world-wide invasion of demon-locusts. In both Exodus and Revelation only unbelievers are the sole object of the plague. While Exodus 10 never explicitly says that Israelites would be exempt from the locust plague, it does say the locusts would come into Pharaoh's territory, fill his house, and finish the destruction that the hail had begun. Since the hail did not come in the land of Goshen where the children of Israel resided and the locusts were to complete the destruction begun by the hail, it is logical to conclude that the Israelites were spared from the locust invasion as well.

How they can strike
The demons from the abyss cannot kill men, but they can make men wish they were dead.

> And to them it was given that they should not kill them, but that they should be tormented five months: and their torment was as the torment of a scorpion, when he striketh

a man. And in those days shall men seek death, and shall not find it; and shall desire to die, and death shall flee from them.

—Rev. 9:5–6

The word used here for "torment" is often used in the Bible of the suffering and pain of hell. Also, notice in verse 5 the first use of the word "as." This word is used a total of nine times in this section to help us understand as best we can in human terms what this entire scenario will be like.

The torment of these demonic beings is like the torment from the sting of a scorpion. I have never been stung by a scorpion, but one day in the field next to our church a small boy was stung on the hand by a small scorpion. He screamed bloody-murder for an hour straight. He was totally inconsolable for the first thirty minutes. Just think of enduring that kind of pain for five months without relief. It will drive men stark-raving mad. It will drive them to suicide, but according to Revelation 9:6 they will not be able to even take their own lives to stop the excruciating pain.

Charles Ryrie describes the insanity this pain will produce and man's inability to terminate the torment.

> The effect of this torment is to drive men to suicide, but they will not be able to die. Although men will prefer death to the agony of living, death will not be possible. Bodies will not sink and drown; poisons and pills will have no effect; and somehow even bullets and knives will not do their intended job.
>
> —Ryrie, *Revelation*, 62

Imagine the agony and desperation of wanting to commit suicide but finding it impossible. Imagine a gun that won't fire, poison that is ineffective, a leap from a tall building that is interrupted by an invisible safety net, or a rope that will not strangle. Not even Dr. Kevorkian will be able to help. Unbelievable days, indeed.

How long they can strike

The third limitation God places on this invading armada is how long they can inflict their misery on man. The time of torment is specifically limited to five months. I call this time period "five months of hell on earth." The time period is stated twice for emphasis (vv. 5,10). It's interesting that five months (May–September) is the normal season of pillaging for locusts. This is the only judgment in the book of Revelation that is specifically limited to a particular period of time.

Demon Description

The description of these "alien" invaders is fiercesome.

> And the shapes of the locusts were like unto horses prepared unto battle; and on their heads were as it were crowns like gold, and their faces were as the faces of men. And they had hair as the hair of women, and their teeth were as the teeth of lions. And they had breastplates, as it were breastplates of iron; and the sound of their wings was as the sound of chariots of many horses running to battle. And they had tails like unto scorpions, and there were stings in their tails: and their power was to hurt men five months.
>
> —Rev. 9: 7–10

Notice that the chief characteristic of these invaders is that they are "locusts." As we have already seen, these are not actual locusts, but demonic beings with the appearance of locusts. It's interesting to me that in all the alien movies I have ever seen, the aliens always have a locust-like appearance, at least in the face and head. The head and eyes have a locust-like, insect-like look—dark, slanted eyes and a head that is wide at the top and narrow at the bottom.

I was amazed in the movie *Independence Day* to discover that the beings in that movie mirror almost exactly the description of the demonic invaders described in Revelation 9. In one powerful scene near the end of the movie, the President of the United States is observing one of the alien beings that is being contained in Area 51 in Nevada. The being somehow communicates telepathically with the President. He grabs his head in pain and says, "They are like locusts, they move from one area to another devouring everything in their path." The alien invaders in the last days described in Revelation are also like locusts and they too will pillage everything in their path.

While these beings are "like locusts" overall, they have eight other characteristics that are listed.

1. like horses
2. crowns on their heads (like gold)
3. faces like the faces of men
4. long hair like the hair of women
5. teeth like lions (denoting their voracity)
6. covering like breastplates of iron (like a heavy body armor). This reveals that they are well-protected. Man is helpless against their onslaught.
7. sound like chariots or horses going to battle as they move
8. tails like scorpions

In each case the word *like* indicates that a comparison is being made and that something other than a literal description is intended. This doesn't mean these beings are not literal, but that John is describing them the best he can by comparing them to things that are familiar. This litany gives another way to list the specific description of these locusts from hell.

heads: crowns like gold
faces: like men's
hair: like women's
teeth: like lion's
breastplates: like iron
wings: like the sound of chariots with many horses
tails: like scorpions

One of my friends, when he read this description, said that it sounded like a description of a rock star. Just think of the unbelievable appearance of these invaders from the abyss. They are long-haired, horse-shaped, flying locusts with scorpion tails and golden crowns above human faces covered with skin like a coat of armor. They are a kind of "infernal cherubim"—a combination of the horse, the man, the woman, the lion, the scorpion, and the locust. Their size is not given, but they are cleary much larger that ordinary locusts.

The sound made by the wings of these agents of misery is the loud rushing sound of a swarm. This sound creates a formidable psychological problem and implies the hopelessness of resisting them (Thomas, 2:37). Joel compares the noise of locusts' wings to the clatter and clangor of chariot wheels and the hoofbeat of horses moving swiftly into battle (Joel 2:4–5; cf. 2 Kings 7:6; Jer. 47:3). The same scene is described here.

"To See or Not To See"

One question that I have been asked about this passage is whether these demonic beings will be visible or invisible when they invade the Earth. Since demons are spirit beings, many conclude that these demons from the abyss will be invisible to the natural eye. While one should not be overly dogmatic, it seems best to view these demon-locusts as visible at least some of the time. The way their physical characteristices are described in detail and the fact that they darken the sun when they erupt from the abyss seems to indicate a material, physical, visible form. Of course, it is possible that since demons are spirit beings they can go back and forth from material and visible to immaterial and invisible.

However, the key issue is not whether these beings are visible or invisible, but rather whether they are real. And this passage clearly reveals that these beings are real and that their venom will afflict the entire unbelieving world with unimaginable horror and agony.

The Terminator

The leader or king of this alien invasion is the angel of the abyss. His name in Hebrew is Abaddon, and in Greek is Apollyon (Rev. 9:11) which means "Destroyer" or "Terminator." His title is expressive of the destruction to be brought about by the demonic hosts this angel leads.

Some have identified this king of the abyss as Satan himself; however, Satan's domain is the heavenly places, not the underworld. Satan has no connection with the abyss in Scripture until He is cast there in Revelation 20:1–3. It is better to identify this king as an unnamed, unidentified fallen angel who is in charge of the abyss. He could be described as Satan's hellish "Michael the Archangel." This terrifying terminator will lead the satanic special forces in their all-out invasion of planet Earth in the last days.

One Down, Two to Go

The description of the coming alien invasion of Earth is so bizarre I feel like I need to stop and catch my breath after reading Revelation 9:1–11. The scene is surreal and unimaginable in its horror. But as bad as it is, it's only the beginning of the alien invasion of planet Earth in the last days. "One woe is past; and, behold, there come two woes more hereafter" (Rev. 9:12).

Believe it or not, the worst is yet to come!

Chapter Thirteen

The Empire Strikes Back

Crown Him the Lord of Years
The Potentate of Time
Creator of the rolling spheres
Ineffably sublime
                    —*Crown Him with Many Crowns*

In almost all the alien adventure movies, there is a sequel—a part two. Think about all the sequels—*Alien 2, Star Trek* (I think the total is up to five now), and of course, my favorite, the *Star Wars* trilogy, especially the second movie, *The Empire Strikes Back*. In all of these series, in the initial installment the bad guys invade and are temporarily driven back, only to appear again in a more powerful, aggressive, nefarious form in the sequel.

In Revelation 9 the same basic scenario is present: the aliens from the abyss invade and wreak their havoc for five months and then are cut off by the invisible hand of God. However, this is not the end of the story. There is a sequel, and like all good sequels, the enemy is back and badder than ever. This second last-days alien invasion in Revelation is called the second woe and the sixth trumpet judgment.

Woe #2

Revelation 9:13–21 reveals the judgment of God at the blowing of the sixth trumpet judgment. As we have seen, the fifth trumpet judgment will empty the abyss and demonic scorpion–locusts will be unleashed on the Earth to torment men for five months.

The sixth trumpet judgment of the last days, or the second woe as it is also called, records the second phase or sequel of the alien invasion of Earth.

Angels of Death

When the sixth angel sounds, he hears the voice of God commanding him to "loose the four angels which are bound in the great river Euphrates" (Rev. 9:14). While every other occurrence of the word "angel" in Revelation refers to elect or unfallen angels (except for the references to human messengers in Rev. 2–3), the context here makes it clear that these four angels are fallen angels who have been kept bound until the divinely appointed time for them to perform their task as agents of God. The fact that they are "bound" clearly identifies them as fallen angels. Nowhere in Scripture are holy angels bound, but in Jude 6 some wicked angels are bound.

It's interesting that these evil angels are bound at the Euphrates River. There are many theories about the significance of this location. Some would give it a purely symbolic meaning. Others believe it is literal and is mentioned here because the Euphrates formed the easternmost boundary beyond which evil came upon the ancient world via Assyria and Babylon. Still others believe it is referenced because the area of the Euphrates was the birthplace of evil among men since the Euphrates flowed through the Garden of Eden (Gen. 2:10–14), and since ancient Babel was on the Euphrates (Gen. 11). Others, who believe ancient Babylon will be rebuilt in the last days, see significance in the fact that these angels are bound there. Some who believe in a future rebuilt Babylon also believe it will be the capital city of the Antichrist.

Many students of Bible prophecy associate the mention of the Euphrates here in Revelation 9:14 with Revelation 16:12 and the drying up of the Euphrates to prepare the way for the kings of the East to gather at Armageddon.

Whatever the specific reason for the mention of the Euphrates, I believe it must be taken literally in this context as the place where this deadly quartet is bound until God is ready to use them as agents of His wrath and fury.

The Potentate of Time

Revelation 9:15 reveals God's absolute, total control and sovereignty over time. The infinite Creator who exists outside time and who created time, nevertheless works within time to carry out His program for this world.

Notice the specificity and precision in verse 15: "And the four angels were loosed, which were prepared for an hour, and a day, and a month, and a year. . . ." The four angels are in a state of preparedness and readiness awaiting the divinely appointed time to begin their nefarious task. Even though they are fallen angels, they are still the divinely appointed and prepared agents to carry out the will of God at the appointed moment. They cannot act without express divine command.

God has the time for this event narrowed down to the very year, month, day, and hour. Before the world was hung in space, God had appointed a specific hour for this sixth trumpet to sound and for these fallen angels to swing into action to fulfill His plan. Our God is in sovereign control over all the events of this world down to the very moment of their occurrence, including every event in your life and mine. All the world is on God's time schedule.

I love the final verse of the old hymn, *Crown Him with Many Crowns.*

> Crown Him the Lord of Years
> The Potentate of Time
> Creator of the rolling spheres
> Ineffably sublime

The Alien Armada

Revelation 9:16 reveals that a massive armada of horsemen numbering 200 million will be unleashed on the Earth at the sounding of the sixth trumpet or second woe. The number 200 million is literally "a double myriad of myriads." This will be the most numerous and invincible army ever assembled. But who or what is this army? Is this army composed of humans or demons?

Students of prophecy down through the centuries have interpreted this as referring to the Turkish cavalry, the Moslem conquests, and about every other human cavalcade in history. Many other sound scholars believe that his army of 200 million is a human army and they relate it to the "kings of the east" in Revelation 16:12–16 who cross the dried-up Euphrates

River and gather at Armageddon. In favor of this interpretation, they cite the similarities between Revelation 9:13–16 and 16:12–16, that the modern nations of the Orient could amass an army of this size, and the description of the weapons in Revelation 9:17–19 as similar to a scene of modern warfare.

> And thus I saw the horses in the vision, and them that sat on them, having breastplates of fire, and of jacinth, and brimstone: and the heads of the horses were as the heads of lions; and out of their mouths issued fire and smoke and brimstone. By these three was the third part of men killed, by the fire, and by the smoke, and by the brimstone, which issued out of their mouths. For their power is in their mouth, and in their tails: for their tails were like unto serpents, and had heads, and with them they do hurt.

Those who view this as a human army see John as describing modern warfare in the best words that he can with his limited vocabulary in the first century. They picture this language as describing modern tanks, artillery, and helicopters. Ray Stedman advocates this view.

> What does this description mean? It hardly seems possible that John himself understood what he was looking at. All he could do was record his impressions of future warriors, armor, and weaponry far beyond his ability to imagine. In fact, the events described in this ancient book of prophecy are still in our own future, and thus may be beyond our ability to imagine as well.
>
> Yet it seems clear that what John envisions for us is the machinery of modern (or future) military destruction translated into the military terminology of his own day. Breastplates of various colors seems to suggest armored chariots—that is, tanks, troop carriers, missile launchers, rocket batteries, artillery pieces, and aircraft of various countries bearing the identifying colors of their nations of origin. Since there are so many nations gathered, it would

be necessary that each nation's war material be clearly identified.

The lion's mouths which spouted fire and smoke suggests cannons, mortars, rocket launchers, and even missiles killing great masses of people with fire, radiation, and even poison gases. The fact that one-third of the human race is destroyed in this conflict strongly suggests that weapons of mass destruction, including nuclear weapons, will be used.

Another intriguing image is that of the horses' tails, described as being like snakes, having heads that inflict injury. These words could apply to various kinds of modern armament—helicopter gunships with rotors mounted on their long tail assemblies, or perhaps missiles which leave a snake-like trail of smoke in their wake and inflict injury with their warheads. Perhaps it is a description of weapons that are yet to be invented.

Regardless of what the details of these future images mean, the overall picture is clear—and frightening. This last and greatest of all military campaigns will result in monstrous slaughter on an unbelievable scale.

—Stedman, *God's Final Word*, 194–95

While this view is possible, I believe it is better to view this massive army as an army of demonic invaders. There are six main reasons I prefer this view. First, the fifth and sixth trumpets go together since they are the first two of the three woes. The fifth trumpet describes demons who torment unsaved people for a limited period of time. The sixth trumpet seems to carry this same judgment forward to an intensified level where another group of demons are unleashed to slaughter the inhabitants of the Earth.

Second, this armada is led by fallen angels just like the fifth trumpet.

Third, the fearsome description in verses 17–19 fits supernatural beings much better than modern warfare.

Fourth, the emphasis is on the horses in these verses and not the riders. As Robert Thomas says:

> The fact that the horses rather than the riders are the destructive agents and that they and their riders wear brightly colored breastplates matching the destructive forces proceeding from their mouths suggests that the combination of horse and rider is of superhuman origin.
>
> —*Revelation*, 2:46

Fifth, there are other examples in the Scripture of supernatural armies of cavalry. Horses of fire took Elijah up to heaven (2 Kings 2:11). Horses and chariots of fire protected Elisha at Dothan (2 Kings 6:13–17). Heavenly horses and horsemen from the celestial realm introduce the reign of Christ (Rev. 19:14). It seems logical that Satan would resist the coming of that kingdom with his own infernal cavalry.

Sixth, the weapons that are mentioned—fire, brimstone, and smoke—are always supernatural weapons in the Bible and are associated with hell four times in Revelation (14:10–11; 19:20; 20:10; 21:8).

For these reasons we believe the sounding of the sixth trumpet signals the onslaught of another demonic invasion of Earth. But this time the invasion is by squadrons of demonic cavalry—hellish horsemen riding satanic steeds!

Hellish Horsemen

The scene in Revelation 9:17–19 is horrifying, ghastly, and revolting. It makes Hollywood's most terrifying special effects look tame. It makes George Lucas look like a bumbling amateur. This passage records the future invasion of Earth by 200 million fire-breathing monsters from the underworld.

> And thus I saw the horses in the vision, and them that sat on them, having breastplates of fire, and of jacinth, and brimstone: and the heads of the horses were as the heads of

lions; and out of their mouths issued fire and smoke and brimstone. By these three was the third part of men killed, by the fire, and by the smoke, and by the brimstone, which issued out of their mouths. For their power is in their mouth, and in their tails: for their tails were like unto serpents, and had heads, and with them they do hurt.

The mention of horses in the Bible usually signals warfare. These horses are no exception. The mention of the riders' breastplates probably refers to the breastplates of the horses as well, since the description focuses on the horses. In ancient times horses are known to have worn such apparel.

The breastplates are the color of fire, jacinth, and brimstone. The word for fire is the Greek word *purinous* which represents a fiery red color. Jacinth is a dark-shaded color including that of sulphurous smoke. Brimstone describes something made of sulphur with a sulphurous, or light yellow, hue. Brimstone is often associated with the wrath of God in the Bible. The three colors mentioned here denote the relationship of these horses to the lake of fire and also recall the fate of Sodom and Gomorrah in Genesis 19:24,28. Just as God destroyed the cities of the plain for their wickedness near the beginning of time, He will destroy one-third of the Earth for its wickedness at the end of the age.

The horses' heads are like the those of lions which carries the idea of majesty, terror, ferocity, and destructiveness.

The most destructive aspect of these horses is their mouths which emit "fire, smoke and brimstone." These horses are fire-breathing monsters from hell.

The Day a Billion People Died

The demonic invasion under the fifth trumpet brings unbearable judgment on the world, but the invaders can only torment men for five months; they could not take life. However, under the sixth trumpet this restriction is removed and this infernal army now massacres one-third of the human race—

the largest death-toll in human history up to that point. Man has no weapon against them! This isn't Hollywood where man always comes up with some way through his own ingenuity to defeat the invaders. In this last-days invasion man is utterly helpless and hopeless to help himself against these creatures that are hell-bent on genocide.

One-fourth of the Earth has already been slain by the fourth seal (Rev. 6:8). That's at least one billion people. Now one-third is killed, meaning another billion die. At this point over one-half of the world's population has been decimated.

But all of this carnage brings man to his senses and to his knees in submission before his Creator—right? WRONG!

The Saddest Verse in the Bible

What is the response of the survivors of this decimation? Total unrepentance and intensified rebellion. Man's response to this destruction is open defiance. The total depravity of man is nowhere more evident than in this verse. This same response is elicited from man's sinful heart in Revelation 16:10–11.

> And the fifth angel poured out his vial upon the seat of the beast; and his kingdom was full of darkness; and they gnawed their tongues for pain, And blasphemed the God of heaven because of their pains and their sores, and repented not of their deeds.

These verses are the clearest illustration in the Bible of the truth of Jeremiah 17:9: "The heart is deceitful above all things and desperately wicked: who can know it?"

The Salvation Army

You must be wondering at this point if there is any hope for this Earth and mankind. The intensity and scope of the destruction is staggering. This looks like the end. Is there any way of escape? Can man be saved from this scourge? Will these demonic aliens take over the world?

The answer is found in the REAL Independence Day!

Chapter Fourteen

The REAL Independence Day

*And then shall appear the sign of the Son
of man in heaven: and then shall all the
tribes of the earth mourn, and they shall
see the Son of man coming in the clouds of
heaven with power and great glory*

—Matthew 24:30

During the Fourth of July weekend in 1996 a blockbuster hit the big screen—a movie that seemed to hit home with the collective psyche of the modern American. The TV ads before the release of the movie showed a spaceship the size of a city hovering ominously over the White House and then blowing it to smithereens with a single blast from its alien ray cannon. The size of the spaceships, the sites targeted for destruction and the apocalyptic nature of the annihilation all played heavily into Judgment Day eschatology.

The theme of this movie, like most of the other "alien invasion" movies before it, was man's ability to overcome the hopeless situation by using his own intellect, ingenuity, and courage. In the movie, man appears totally helpless before the vastly superior firepower of the invaders. The major cities of the world are being systematically and successively destroyed. But just when it appears that all hope is gone, a longshot, last ditch plan is devised and in the end man is the great victor over the wicked forces of alien life. Throughout the movie there is even well-placed humor and the main characters have quite a bit of swagger.

The entire movie is a celebration of the greatness of man and is really about man's independence from God. Man can solve his own problems, especially over these aliens, and certainly doesn't need divine deliverance. An article from *World* magazine (July 20/27, 1996) aptly summarizes an important message in the movie *Independence Day*.

> Another implied message of *Independence Day* is there is no God. Aliens have sent fifteen-mile-long space ships to perch over major cities of the world—yet no one thinks to pray.
>
> In the 1950s movie *When Worlds Collide*, danger

brought the nations of the earth to their knees, but in this movie the only character who thinks about God as a possible help is a non-practicing Jew. When he finally prays, it is in a humorous scene where tolerant inclusiveness is more the point than rescue.

Lest we think prayer is what undergirds the final victory, the movie's ending deliberately has man, not God, wiping out the aliens.

Indepenence Day is humanistically optimistic, celebrating the ability of human beings to use creativity to protect themselves and thereby declare an independence day from God.

Men in Black

Another recent alien movie that focuses on man's ability to control alien invaders is the action-packed movie *MIB* (*Men in Black*). The advertisement hails the skill of these alien-busters. When the aliens invade, don't call the FBI, forget the CIA, call the MIB; they are the only ones who can control the situation. Once again, the whole issue is one great big laughing matter, as the aliens are no match for man's ingenuity and power. The MIB pull out their big alien-busting hand cannons and blow the evil aliens away. Will Smith and Tommy Lee Jones, the two lead actors, have the situation in hand.

However, as we have already seen, when the real "alien" invasion of Earth occurs in the last days, man will be totally impotent to do anything to extricate himself from the power and malevolence of these invaders. Man's only hope will be found in help from on high. God in His mercy and grace will send a Deliverer to rescue fallen man—the same Deliverer who came two thousand years ago to deliver us from our sins. Who is this Deliverer? He is the King of kings and the Lord of lords, the Lord Jesus Christ.

Hallelujah!

When Handel wrote his classic *Messiah*, the crowning piece

was the "Hallelujah Chorus" which is based on Revelation 11:15 when Jesus Christ returns from heaven to take His rightful place on the throne to reign forever and ever. Revelation 11:14–15 records the sounding of the seventh trumpet—the announcement of the third woe. The fifth trumpet, or first woe, brought the demonic horde from the abyss. The sixth trumpet, or second woe, called forth the 200 million horsemen from hell. The seventh trumpet, or third woe, announces the coming of the Lord Jesus Christ to rescue planet Earth from destruction. It celebrates the REAL Independence Day when the world is delivered by Jesus Christ from certain destruction.

> The second woe is past; and, behold, the third woe cometh quickly. And the seventh angel sounded; and there were great voices in heaven, saying, The kingdoms of this world are become the kingdoms of our Lord, and of his Christ; and he shall reign for ever and ever.
>
> —Rev 11:14–15

Many other passages of scripture describe the REAL Independence Day when Christ returns.

> And then shall appear the sign of the Son of man in heaven: and then shall all the tribes of the earth mourn, and they shall see the Son of man coming in the clouds of heaven with power and great glory
>
> —Matt 24:30

> The Lord Jesus shall be revealed from heaven with his mighty angels.
>
> —2 Thess 1:7

> Behold, he cometh with clouds; and every eye shall see him.
>
> —Rev 1:7

Revelation 19:11–16 provides the most graphic description of the scene of victory, triumph, conquest, and majesty when the Creator comes back to His Creation.

> And I saw heaven opened, and behold a white horse; and he that sat upon him was called Faithful and True, and in righteousness he doth judge and make war. His eyes were as a flame of fire, and on his head were many crowns; and he had a name written, that no man knew, but he himself. And he was clothed with a vesture dipped in blood: and his name is called The Word of God. And the armies which were in heaven followed him upon white horses, clothed in fine linen, white and clean. And out of his mouth goeth a sharp sword, that with it he should smite the nations: and he shall rule them with a rod of iron: and he treadeth the winepress of the fierceness and wrath of Almighty God. And he hath on his vesture and on his thigh a name written, KING OF KINGS, AND LORD OF LORDS.

This is an event everyone can see. The Lord Himself riding on a white stallion will come to rescue this embattled planet from destruction.

"Veni, vidi, vici"?

In 47 B.C., the Roman army under Julius Caesar soundly defeated the forces of King Pharnaces, who fought the Romans for control of the kingdom of Pontus in Asia Minor. After his victory, Caesar returned to Rome and made his famous announcement, "Veni, vidi, vici," "I came, I saw, I conquered."

Some seventeen hundred years later a Polish military strategist, King John III Sobieski, led a brilliant campaign to drive the Ottoman invaders out of central Europe. Leading a force of 25,000 men, he came to the aid of the German emperor Leopold I and beat the invaders back from the walls of Vienna, saving the city and the emperor. The Polish king was given an audience before Pope Innocent XI, who congratulated him on his victory.

King John's reply was: "I came, I saw, *God* conquered."

So shall it be in the last days. God will destroy the evil forces of hell and the wicked armies of the Earth at the triumphal return of Christ. At this time the minions of hell will be bound in the abyss with Satan (Rev. 20:1–3) and will ultimately be consigned to the lake of fire forever (Rev. 20:10).

The Lord will come, the world will see, and God will conquer.

What Will You Do with Jesus?

This chapter raises a very important question that every person reading these words must confront: What will you do with Jesus? His coming is the fulcrum of human history. All hope for this broken, dying, disintegrating world flows from the fact that He is coming again. He is coming as King of kings and Lord of lords. The key question for each reader to face is: What will you do with Jesus?

And what will He do with you?

Chapter Fifteen

The Final Destination

Where'er I go the people say,
"What's the news? What's the news?
What is the order of the day?
What's the news? What's the news?"
Oh, I have got good news to tell.
My Savior has done all things well.
He triumphed over death and hell.

A *New Yorker* cartoon portrays a scene from hell. We see several pudgy, furry devils, with their three-pronged forks and pointed tails, driving throngs of hapless human sinners through the licking flames of the inferno. Sitting on a hot rock observing the scene is a rather reflective gentleman, hand on his chin. He has been down under for some time and knows the scene. Obviously, he has just been quizzed by a rather dazed, innocent-looking gentleman about what it is like farther down into the scorching caverns. As a frowning devil looks over his shoulder at them, the long-term human resident of Hades tells the expectant, hopeful arrival, deflatingly, "No, it's not going to be okay."

Our world, especially in these last days, is desperate for "It's-going-to-be-okay" assurances. The politically correct thing to do is to say, "It's going to be okay." After reading the truths in this book you are probably wanting to hear someone say, "It's going to be okay." But it's not going to be okay. This world is headed for judgment of the most unimaginable scope and severity. The hellish invasion of our planet is just a small part of the overall pounding this world will endure in the days ahead. Things are definitely not going to be okay according to the Book of Revelation. And sometimes it's our job to say to our culture, "Nope, there's bad news before there's good news. The bad news is, things are not going to be okay. But **the good news** is that things can be okay." Yes, there is good news, wonderful news, there is deliverance, and it's found in the person and work of Jesus Christ. These old Welsh words are so true today as people are wondering what is happening in our world.

Where'er I go the people say,
"What's the news? What's the news?

What is the order of the day?

What's the news? What's the news?"

Oh, I have got good news to tell.

My Savior has done all things well.

He triumphed over death and hell.

This is the good news of Jesus Christ! He died on the cross for your sins. He paid your sin debt in full, totally satisfying the holiness and justice of God on your behalf. He was raised from the dead and offers you new life by simple faith and trust in Him. You can receive Him as your Savior right now by acknowledging your sinful condition before Him (Rom. 3:23), by recognizing your total inability to save yourself by any merit or activity of your own (Eph. 2:8–9), and by accepting and receiving Jesus Christ as your Savior from sin (John 1:12). When you receive Him as your Savior, you can be sure of your final destination (1 Pet. 1:3–5). You can be sure that you will spend eternity in heaven with God, the holy angels, and all other men and women who have trusted the Lord for salvation (John 10:27–30). You can be certain that Christ will come and receive you to Himself and deliver you from the wrath to come on this planet (John 14:1–3; 1 Thess. 1:10; Rev. 3:10). Do it now, before it's too late. Trust Christ as your Savior. Call upon His name for salvation, and He will save you. He is your **only** hope for salvation (John 14:6; Acts 4:12).

The choice is yours.

Your Call

Through the pitch-black night, the captain sees a light dead ahead on a collision course with his ship. He sends a signal: "Change your course ten degrees east."

The light signals back: "Change yours, ten degrees west."

Angry, the captain sends: "I'm a Navy captain! Change your course, sir!"

"I'm a seaman, second class," comes the reply. "Change your course, sir."

Now the captain is furious. "I'm a battleship! I'm not changing course!"

There's one last reply. "I'm a lighthouse. Your call."

This is often the way it is with sinful man. Man in his arrogance and pride demands that God move—that He conform to us and our desires. But God is the lighthouse, and He will not move. If you do not move, your life will end in shipwreck on the jagged rocks of the judgment of God.

Won't you make the move and receive God's gracious gift of salvation through His Son? It's your call.

Believe in the Lord Jesus Christ and flee the wrath to come!

Appendix A

That Saucer You Saw, Sir!

UFOs have been seen in every size and shape imaginable. Some UFOs have been reported to be the size of Coke cans, while others have been reported to be as large as four-story buildings. Often UFOs appear as spots of light which flutter and dance in sporadic fashion across the night sky. UFOs have been reported in the shape of boomerangs, cubes, spheres, elastic blobs, diamonds, cigars, disks, eggs, triangles, hamburgers, and cones. UFOs have been observed flying solo, in groups of two, and occasionally in large groups. What's more, many witnesses would attest to the enormous effect the "contact" experience had made on their life—some have experienced a religious revitalization; others have been ridiculed and even lost their jobs. Some have suffered from what appeared to be radiation poisoning; others found that they could sleep only with all the lights in the house turned on. Sightees often have a difficult time verbally describing UFOs. UFOs have been called such things as:

"flaming spheres"
"spinning fire disks"
"glowing, whirling wheels"
"celestial medusae"
"hovering, zooming whatzits"
"skyborne somethings"
"magnetic flutterings"
"will-o-the-wisps"
"jack-o-lanterns"
"screaming meemees"

But seriously, how does one go about properly reporting an unidentified flying object? What are the proper classifications? What is the standard grid? The following classification system was developed by ufologist Dr. J. Allen Hynek of the Center for UFO Studies (CUFOS):

Official UFO Classifications

NLs
Nocturnal Lights
These sightings include well-defined lights in the night sky whose appearance and/or motion are not explainable in terms of conventional light sources. The light appears most often as red, blue, orange, or white. These form the largest group of UFO reports.

DDs
Daylight Discs
Daytime sightings are generally oval- or disk-shaped, metallic-appearing objects. They can appear high in the sky or close to the ground, and they are often reported to hover. They can seem to disappear with astounding speed.

RVs
Radar-Visual
Of special significance are unidentified "blips" on radar screens that coincide with and confirm simultaneous visual sightings by the same or other witnesses. These cases are infrequent.

Encounter Meter
The science of ufology currently specifies six distinct categories of sightings. They are as follows:

CE1
Close Encounters of the First Kind
Though the witness observes a UFO nearby, there appears to

be no interaction with either the witness or the environment. The sighting of a UFO at close proximity.

CE2
Close Encounters of the Second Kind
These encounters include details of interaction between the UFO and the environment, which may vary from interference with car ignition systems and electronic gears to imprints or burns on the ground and physical effects of the craft on plants, animals, and humans.

CE3
Close Encounters of the Third Kind
Occupants of a UFO—intelligent entities that are humanlike ("humanoid") or not humanlike—have been reported. There is usually no direct contact or communication with the witness. However, interactions between human "contactees" and UFO occupants can fall into this category. In addition to the two distinctives already mentioned under Close Encounters of the First and Second Kind there is now also a direct confrontation with a space-being.

CE4
Close Encounters of the Fourth Kind
Onboard experiences or abductions of individuals or people, usually in the presence of "humanoids." This classification was added recently, as reports of incidents involving very close contact—even detainment of witnesses—have increased. The contactee is abducted by the UFO occupants, taken aboard the landed craft, and subjected to a variety of "tests" and "experiments." Some investigators claim to have recovered physical evidence of these interactions in the form of scars from alien surgical incisions. Some abductees report memories of devices being implanted within their bodies, typically through the nose.

CE5
Close Encounters of the Fifth Kind
Contact with alien life forms through metaphysical means—personal contact with UFO entities through metaphysical or other occult means.

CE6
Close Encounters of the Sixth Kind
Injury or death resulting from a UFO close encounter.

CE7
Close Encounters of the Seventh Kind
This new category heading, coined by the authors of this book, refers to the final manifestation and all-out invasion of demonic/alien beings onto planet Earth.

About the Authors

Mark Hitchcock holds a B.S. from Oklahoma State University; a J.D. from Oklahoma City University School of Law; and a Th.M. from Dallas Theological Seminary. Mark is currently a Ph.D. candidate at Dallas Theological Seminary, and is the pastor of Faith Bible Church in Edmond, Oklahoma. Mark and his wife, Cheryl, have two sons, Justin and Samuel.

Scot Overbey holds a B.S. from the University of Arkansas; an M.B.A. from Oklahoma City University; and a Th.M. from Dallas Theological Seminary. Scot is the associate pastor of Faith Bible Church in Edmond, Oklahoma. Scot and his wife, Kym, have five children, Nathan, Anna Ruth, John Scot, George, and Grace.